# BUILD YOUR FAMILY BANK

Emily Griffiths-Hamilton

# BUILD YOUR FAMILY BANK

## A Winning Vision for Multigenerational Wealth

**Figure.1**
*Vancouver*

Cataloguing data available from Library and Archives Canada
ISBN 978-1-927958-07-0 (cloth)
ISBN 978-1-927958-05-6 (ebook)
ISBN 978-1-927958-06-3 (pdf)

Editing by Barbara Pulling
Copy editing by Pam Robertson
Jacket and interior design by Jessica Sullivan
Jacket photograph: Susanne Kürth / Source: PHOTOCASE
Printed and bound in Canada by Friesens
Distributed in the U.S. by Publishers Group West

Figure 1 Publishing Inc.
Vancouver BC Canada
www.figure1pub.com

*To my husband, Paul, and
our sons, David and Brandon.*

*For all that you have taught me,
are teaching me,
and will continue to teach me.*

*I treasure you all.*

# CONTENTS

Your Legacy

Accountants can't create it,
Lawyers can't litigate it,
Governments can't legislate it,
Professors can't teach it.

Only you can orchestrate it!

DONALD MACKENZIE
*corporate consultant, Mebhin Consultancy Inc.*

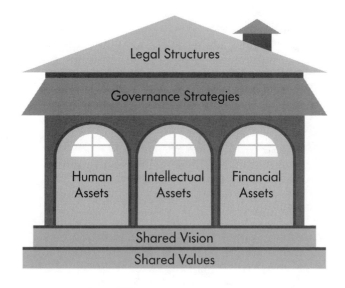

THE FAMILY BANK

# INTRODUCTION:
## A Secret No More

T HERE IS no better time than now to unlock the secrets
behind successful succession and wealth-transition plans.
Through research conducted over the past decade, we have
gained new insight into why some families achieve successful
multigenerational succession and wealth transitions and why
others don't. Well, as Spanish novelist Miguel de Cervantes
wrote in *Don Quixote*, "Forewarned, forearmed; to be prepared is
half the victory." By reading this book, you will be forewarned
about why (and at what rate) most professionally advised succession and wealth-transition plans fail, and then forearmed
with a successful solution: the Family Bank approach.

I arrive at the subject of succession and wealth-transition
plans with three generations of experience. My maternal
grandfather was the veterinarian Dr. William Ballard, one of
Canada's greatest success stories in terms of dynamic wealth
creation. Beginning in the depths of the Great Depression, he
came up with a high-quality formula for dog food and then
canned it for easier distribution. Canned dog food may seem
like an obvious idea today, but my grandfather was at the fore-
front of the industry. My grandfather had four children: three
daughters, one of whom is my mother, and one son. While
he was alive, his financial assets were managed in a way that
stewarded them for the benefit of future generations. When

he died, the business passed to his son, as was typical of the era, and each daughter was bequeathed liquid assets. My grandfather also established trusts for each of his grandchildren.

My parents, as second-generation inheritors, also became dynamic wealth creators themselves. My father, Frank A. Griffiths, built a successful career in public accounting alongside his father, who was also a chartered accountant. At the same time, my father was building a sports and media empire. He and his partners began with the acquisition of the Vancouver, B.C., radio station CKNW. As the transaction was nearing a close, additional financing was required, and my parents secured that by way of a loan from my grandparents' Family Bank. In this way, two elements of what I call the Family Bank approach were set in motion: successful multigenerational wealth transition requires that the family's financial capital be recirculated as loans from the Family Bank, rather than depleted through handouts with no expected repayment, and the need for each generation to work.

I am a third-generation inheritor, not just of financial wealth but more importantly of bedrock values passed down through my family from generation to generation. As the result of a complex corporate restructuring in my family, I received a substantial inheritance in my early thirties, in the form of ownership in a National Hockey League team and a privately owned state-of-the-art arena to which my partners and I added a National Basketball Association franchise. As a young inheritor, I was perhaps better prepared than many to maintain control of my inheritance. My core values, passed down from my family, protected me from foolish expenditures, and I had already undertaken work entirely independent of my family, earning a living as a chartered accountant like my father and grandfather before me. Through my professional training, I acquired the foundational knowledge that protected me from financial incompetence or mismanagement.

Despite this, a cover story entitled "The Griffiths Family Saga: Line of Dissent," published in the May 1997 issue of the *Financial Post Magazine,* suggested that my father had had no succession plan in place when he died in 1994. But as a family insider, I can assure you that my father, a highly successful businessman and professional accountant, had most assuredly put in place a comprehensive succession plan, using the tools available to his generation—the same tools families commonly use today, with the same failed results.

Today, my husband and I are not only the parents of two sons, but also business partners. Our purpose in life, outside of our family, is providing excellent service to our clients. My personal passion involves helping families establish successful succession and wealth-transition plans, drawing on my own personal experience, my professional expertise, as both a chartered accountant (CA) and an Investment Advisor, and what I have learned and assimilated from extensive research compiled over the last decade. To that end, I have made it a goal to read everything on the subject, and use my knowledge to assist others. No family should have to see their name headlined in the national media the way ours was.

The Family Bank concept is not new. As James E. Hughes Jr. explains in his book *Family Wealth: Keeping It in the Family,* successful families have been using the Family Bank approach for generations. As Hughes rightly points out, a family's wealth is not limited to its financial assets but includes its arguably more important forms of wealth: its human and intellectual assets. That means a family's total assets are far greater than its financial assets alone. In this sense, you really are much richer than you think.

The Family Bank approach recognizes that the traditional method of succession and wealth-transition planning, which focuses on controlling financial assets and minimizing and deferring taxes, gets the order of the work backwards. The

Family Bank approach, in contrast, pays close attention to the human elements of the family, then explores governance strategies and considers legal structures that meet the family's needs.

The failure rate today for succession and wealth-transition plans is an astounding 70 percent. Reading this book, you will learn the primary reasons behind that failure rate and how the Family Bank approach is designed specifically to address them. You will discover how to build your own Family Bank, beginning with the solid foundation of your family's shared values and vision. You will learn how to assess all of your family's assets—human, intellectual, and financial—and how to prepare succeeding generations so they can steward those assets successfully. By implementing these strategies, you will be able to craft a succession and wealth-transition plan that truly meets your needs.

The Family Bank is a dynamic approach to multigenerational wealth transitions that can be implemented at any stage in a family's life cycle. For illustrative purposes, I include general guidelines about how and when you might establish a Family Bank, but creating a framework that will suit your particular situation is what you and your family will do together. My work in succession and wealth-transition planning has shown me time and again that each Family Bank is as unique as each family. Also, adopting this approach is not an all or nothing proposition—as you read, you can certainly cherry-pick the information and take away useful tips that resonate with your family's circumstance. Whether you want to implement all of my strategies or only a few is up to you. Practical, concrete, and simply applied, the Family Bank approach unlocks the secrets behind succession and wealth-transition planning, making them accessible to everyone.

# 1

# WHY SUCCESSION
# PLANS FAIL

I READ SOMEWHERE recently that the average entrepreneur spends approximately eighty thousand hours building their business or career and then only eight to ten hours on succession planning. That statement stopped me in my tracks. Could it be true? I wondered. From my very rough calculations, based on a forty-year career and a forty-hour work week, needing eighty thousand hours to build a successful business or career seems, if anything, on the low side—and many people work more than forty hours per week. Yet I also know firsthand that the eight to ten hours estimated for the time spent on succession and wealth-transition planning may well be high!

Many families, especially those with no lawyers, accountants, or financial planners in their ranks, turn their attention to personal financial matters mainly when tax season is upon them. During the consultation for their year-end tax filings, the family's accountant will quite rightly inquire if the family's will and estate plans are up to date. If this question hits a family at a pivotal point in their history, it may spur them into action. If not, they may have good intentions to deal with the issues at hand but let the matter slip for yet another year.

Here's what happened to one family I work with. As a result of proactive nudging by their accountant and personal discussions with business associates of the same age while in their forties, the parents in this family began attending free seminars on succession and wealth transition. They were in their early sixties by the time they came to consult with me. At the start of our second meeting, the father presented me with a bulging reusable grocery bag. For a fleeting moment I was excited, thinking the bag contained treats of some kind—maybe wine. I had to keep my oversized, goofy smile in check when I realized the bag contained documents of some sort. Noticing my facial expression, the father gave a hearty laugh. "I thought you might be interested in this stuff," he said. I continued to smile politely, but no doubt my face resembled a giant question mark. My client continued: "We've attended 'free and not so free' succession and wealth-transition planning seminars for the last twenty years. This bag contains all the junk we were given to take home."

I was genuine in thanking my client for his thoughtfulness. Luckily, I am one of the few people who would almost prefer a historical collection of estate-planning brochures to a special bottle of wine. I took the bag home and spent the weekend reading every item. It was an eye-opening experience for me.

Even though I am usually utterly riveted by the subject matter, reading that shopping bag full of information was difficult. According to the literature from those seminars, succession planning was a very complicated chore. The seminar presenters were mostly accountants, lawyers, or financial planners, and their advice veered towards elaborate corporate restructuring, highly complex tax strategies, and questionable financial projections, with the advice frequently accompanied by product-pushing, like selling insurance and investment products. Reading from the perspective of an individual considering succession planning, the conclusion was inevitable. I would have to take precious time away from my beloved family and career to do this planning, along with paying significant fees to professionals spouting elaborate mumbo jumbo. No wonder so many people throw in the towel, and just ignore the issue!

Was it any different for families at the other end of the spectrum? I asked myself—those who have family members with professional expertise in the subject? My family of origin was an excellent example. My father, a man who shunned the limelight, attracted media attention like a honeypot attracts bees. In most instances, to be fair, our national media did a good job of capturing his business acumen, his reserved nature, and his genuine concern for his community and family. My father began in business working alongside his own father as a chartered accountant (CA) in public practice. My father went on to have a thriving career as a CA until his retirement from the profession at fifty-eight years of age. By all accounts, he was brilliant with numbers and concepts, and thorough and thoughtful in his approach to every business detail.

My father was also a visionary leader, a man born ahead of his time. He was a pioneer, focusing his entrepreneurial efforts primarily on media and sport organizations at a time when that was uncommon. At the time of his death in 1994 at the age of seventy-eight, he held the controlling interest in the media conglomerate he had built, Western International Communications (WIC), a publicly traded Canadian company. The broadcasting empire included key radio and television stations across Canada and a controlling shareholder interest in Canadian Satellite Communications (Cancom) and Allarcom Pay Television Limited (owners of Super Channel in western Canada), as well as holdings in Family Channel, Studio Post and Transfer, Home Theatre, and Cellular Vision. However, the acquisition that landed my family most firmly in the media's bull's-eye was my father's 1974 purchase of the controlling interest in the Vancouver Canucks of the National Hockey League (NHL). His remarkable accomplishments as both a business leader and a philanthropic leader were recognized with many awards, including inductions into the Canadian Business Hall of Fame, the Hockey Hall of Fame, and the Canadian Association of Broadcasters Hall of Fame.

While I am exceptionally proud of my father, I did not write that last paragraph solely to brag about him. The point I want to make here is that his business success owed nothing to chance. And despite media claims to the contrary, this very successful businessman, knowing he was ill, drew on his professional skill set, which included deep knowledge of the tax code and of corporate structures, to put in place a comprehensive, technically crafted succession plan using the tools available to his generation. After creating a highly complex family corporate structure, the balance of attention was focused on the succession of the family businesses. In the end, though, the succession failed and the family lost control of the broadcasting operations, not entirely because of the structures my father put in place, but in spite of them. Sadly, we are still using those same approaches and structures today and, not surprisingly, they are producing the same disappointing results.

As I noted in my introduction to this book, the failure rate for succession and wealth-transition plans is an astounding 70 percent in each generation. This means that if ten first-generation families execute succession plans, only one of those families will remain in control of the family's assets by the third generation. Here's how it works:

FIRST-GENERATION TRANSITION:

| 10 first-generation families | × | 70% failure rate | = | 7 failed succession plans |

Therefore,

| 10 first-generation families | − | 7 failed transitions | = | 3 successful transitions to the second generation |
|---|---|---|---|---|

**SECOND-GENERATION TRANSITION:**

| 3 remaining second-generation families | × | 70% failure rate | = | 2 failed succession plans |
|---|---|---|---|---|

Therefore,

| 3 second-generation families | − | 2 failed transitions | = | 1 successful transition to the third generation |
|---|---|---|---|---|

**THIRD-GENERATION TRANSITION:**

1 family remains in the position to transfer family assets from the first generation to the fourth generation.

And not only that, but this failure rate has been consistent over thousands of years of recorded history, giving rise to the age-old proverb "shirtsleeves to shirtsleeves in three generations."

It is important to recognize that this is not a uniquely North American dilemma. Variations of this proverb are remarkably consistent across cultures. Some examples from around the globe include "rags to rags," "clogs to clogs," "barn stall to barn stall," and "rice paddy to rice paddy" in three generations. Whether estate plans are created in countries with the lowest possible tax rates or in those with the highest rates, in old world cultures or in newer ones, they are equally likely to fail. In other words, even when paying one's share of taxes in countries that support substantive social safety nets, or in countries with or without estate and inheritance taxes, succession and wealth transitions fail at the same rate.

So, do we have a problem here? The answer is most assuredly yes! Of course, it is difficult to solve a problem without knowing what causes it. Well, I have great news. Business scholars and economists are profoundly aware of the positive financial impact the baby boom generation and their family businesses have had on many economies. However, they are equally concerned about the potential negative impact on these economies if the pattern continues and 70 percent of the succession plans for these family businesses fail. For that reason, lots of energy has been expended trying to discover why this pattern of loss has been so tenacious. Over the past decade or so, their research has yielded some key insights.

Enter authors Roy Williams and Vic Preisser and their 2003 book *Preparing Heirs: Five Steps to a Successful Transition of Family Wealth and Values.* Although Williams had spent over forty years coaching business families around the world, and Preisser had more than thirty-five years of experience in business, government, and education, the two men detected a common thread in their estate and financial planning work. Through observing families over multiple generations, they discovered that the traditionally recommended legal, accounting, and financial succession planning structures were not, on their own, able to abate the "shirtsleeves to shirtsleeves in three generations" scenario.

Through their company, The Williams Group, Williams and Preisser performed specific research in this area. To come up with a relevant sample for their interviews, Williams approached fellow members of The Executive Committee International (TEC), a global organization in which business owners in non-competing businesses gather in smaller groups to learn from one another and from invited guest speakers. Through Williams's association with TEC, The Williams Group facilitated 3,250 candid and confidential conversations with family business owners at different points in their succession plans.

Through these conversations, Williams and Preisser were

able to define what constitutes a failed succession plan. According to their definition, a succession plan is considered to have failed if the next generation involuntarily loses control of the transitioned assets. To clarify, they noted that if a family business is sold and the financial assets are voluntarily redeployed into the financial markets, this is considered a reformatting of those assets, not a failed succession plan. Similarly, if the transitioned financial assets are used for philanthropic purposes, this is considered a voluntary redistribution of those assets. In the words of Williams and Preisser, involuntary losses occur when beneficiaries lose control of their wealth through "foolish expenditures, bad investments, mismanagement, inattention, incompetence, family feuding, or other causes within their control." Ouch!

You might now be thinking, "Enough already, please tell me why it is that 70 percent of the time the next generation involuntarily loses control of the transitioned assets, despite us spending significant time and money with professionals creating a succession plan!" This is where things get really interesting. According to data drawn from The Williams Group's interviews, it was found that "the origins of the 70% failure rate lie within the family itself." Four specific causes were identified, and assigned percentages according to how often they were cited:

60% Breakdown in communication and trust within the family unit
25% Unprepared heirs
12% Lack of mission
3% Failures of professionals

And to truly understand their findings, and what these percentages mean, we need to examine the four causes more closely.

## 1. Breakdown in Communication and Trust Within the Family Unit

When I outline in conversation the primary reasons why succession plans fail, I almost always leave off the part about "... and trust" from "breakdown in communication." This is because I believe trust is implicitly required in order to effectively communicate with anyone, not just family members. To me, there is no ambiguity here. If I am in a conversation with someone who I do not trust, then I will not believe what he or she is saying. The message sender may think they have delivered a clear message but, in my mind, I have disregarded it.

Families can be complicated, though, and having genuine trust within a family is paramount in order to have effective communication. Arguably, we cannot expect to have effective communication or harmony within a family without trust. Trust, as defined in the *Oxford English Dictionary,* is a "firm belief in the reliability, truth, ability, or strength of someone or something." Nice words, but what does trust look like in a family? Well, it is represented by simple acts among family members, like saying what you are going to do and then doing it, having one's actions mirror one's words, seeking to support rather than sabotage other family members, and keeping private family matters private. While families must be honest internally, among family members, being honest with individuals outside the family about anything less than favorable to do with another family member is a very quick way to erode trust with that individual. For instance, when my family lost control of our media operations, the national press certainly paid rapt attention when private family matters were inadvertently not kept private.

Communication itself is a complex subject area, with a minefield of opportunities for explosions. One would perhaps assume that since a significant portion of my maiden family's business was concentrated in the communications industry, we would have had a strong grip on this subject area. But in fact, one business associate close to our family and our business operations commented in jest, "Your maiden family's motto could have been: 'Communications: We sell it! We don't practice it!'" "Indeed," I replied with a polite smile, thinking, "We are not that different from many other families."

Even when you are doing your best to say what you mean, there are still many opportunities for communication to easily break down, such as when a message being delivered is misheard, misunderstood, or misinterpreted by the receiver. For example, recently a business partner of mine, the message sender, had arranged a lunch meeting with one of our business associates, the message receiver. In a shared moment of jocularity, the message sender said to the message receiver something about bringing their Platinum Card. The receiver misinterpreted the message and grabbed a cab to a less-than-desirable part of town in an effort to locate a "gentleman's club" called The Platinum Club. The sender, who was waiting at a respectable restaurant, could not be reached as he had forgotten his cellphone. However, as I was still at my desk, the receiver was able to contact me and with my knowledge of where my business partner was, I was able to redirect the message receiver to the respectable restaurant.

This is an example of how easily communication can break down in the simplest of situations. When it comes to family communications, most of us have had firsthand experience with the confusion and complications that can arise when heated family emotions are involved. Adding financial and complex business matters into the mix as well can easily raise the temperature even higher. The Family Bank approach offers a way for families to handle the uncomfortable conversations that will inevitably arise.

Earning a voice is a key element of the Family Bank; to have a say, each family member must earn a voice in the Family Bank, or be genuinely working towards earning it. The qualifications for earning a voice will be specific to each family. Two points are critical, though: the qualification requirements must be agreed to by all members of the Family Bank, and they must be open to alteration if the need arises. A few of the qualifications a family might require for earning a voice include disagreeing without emotion during family discussions, behaving with respect towards other family members, working towards financial independence, and putting the needs of the family first. (See Chapter 11 for more information on earning a voice in the Family Bank.)

Effective communication in a family does not simply happen. It requires practice and a genuine commitment to the process. As you will see in the chapters that follow, the Family Bank approach offers families many opportunities to develop these skills.

## 2. Unprepared Heirs

"Unprepared heirs" is the second reason Williams and Preisser give for the failure of succession plans. I find this term pretentious, though, and not bold enough. I believe it is critical for every individual, not just heirs, to be prepared for the financial realities of the twenty-first century. Whether someone is responsible for making decisions only about their own financial journey, or is in a position to make important decisions about the financial assets of the Family Bank, learning how to manage finances is an important aspect of human and intellectual development. That does not mean gaining an accounting designation, of course, just developing enough knowledge to competently manage financial affairs. (See Chapter 6 for more information on how to achieve this ability.)

Most people think immediately of children when they hear the word heirs, but guess what? An heir can be anyone we decide is a member of our Family Bank. Families and their Family Banks come in all shapes and sizes. Long gone are the days in which a family was defined as a mom and a dad and their biological children. Each unique family will decide who will be members of its Family Bank. In general, though, in order for the Family Bank to be successful, the Family Bank members will share the same values and vision, have long-term commitments to one another and the Family Bank, and whoever they may be, they must be prepared.

This includes spouses. It is common to come across a situation in which a family's primary income earner has died, leaving their estate to an intelligent, sensible, and well-spoken spouse who has no financial acumen whatsoever. The family's income earner has never shared information about debt (its appropriate role and all its potential consequences), interest rates, financial risk, insurance, or taxes with the surviving spouse. I have witnessed this scenario enough times to raise a warning flag here: it is not only children who lose control of the family's wealth through inattention, incompetence, mismanagement, bad investments, and foolish expenditures. It can be the income earner's lack of foresight and closed-off approach to the family regarding the family's finances that cause problems down the road.

Money matters used to be much more straightforward. No serious financial education was necessary, because people could not spend more than they made. When your bank account reached zero, you were done. You had no more money to spend. You were broke, finished, finito! Isn't it remarkable how complicated financial matters have become over the last few decades? Isn't it interesting how we seldom hear that someone is "broke" anymore? Instead, we hear about how indebted people are. How has this shift happened?

There are many reasons for the dramatic change, not the least of which has been our record-low level of interest rates. But perhaps more importantly, for some families money is the last taboo topic.

I recently listened to a radio interview with a well-educated, articulate professional who had written a book about how he ended up filing for personal bankruptcy. What caught my attention was that this man had believed, because he had an excellent job with good cash flow, that he could still afford the trappings of the legacy lifestyle he enjoyed as a child.

Clearly, this man's family had not used the Family Bank approach. If they had, the Family Bank leaders would have explained to family members how the family's lifestyle was being supported. But by avoiding the subject, his family leaders missed many opportunities to teach them financial lessons, such as the fact that the cost of owning an asset does not end with its purchase price, since some assets require additional funds for maintenance and operating costs, or that there are different ways to use credit to finance a family's lifestyle. By stressing the importance of trust and open communication within a family, the Family Bank approach provides a way for families to make conversations about financial realities practical, not emotional.

In addition, the Family Bank approach lets individual family members develop their financial skill sets to objectively separate financial fact from financial fiction. It really is a financial jungle out there. If you prepare all of your Family Bank members well, they will enjoy swinging from tree to tree rather than be left hanging.

### 3. Lack of Mission

Williams and Preisser identified "lack of mission" as the third reason that succession plans fail. Again, in my opinion, an essential element is missing in this phrase. The failure, as they do point out, is caused by not only the lack of a mission but also the lack of a *commonly consented to* mission. In other words, the family in question had not crafted a vision for the future that was shared by all those whom it would affect.

Having a shared mission, purpose, and vision is fundamental to the successful development of your Family Bank. In this exciting world, where nothing remains the same for long, the Family Bank approach is built on a family's realistic, unique vision of itself. This shared vision positively addresses the future of both individual family members and the family as a whole. Without a clear, agreed-upon vision, a family and its members are like a house built on quicksand, one step away from sinking. By contrast, a shared vision that encompasses the personal desires of all of the individual Family Bank members and their dreams for the Family Bank itself will create a solid foundation for the family's future success.

It is impossible to overstate the power of a shared vision. When people's dreams and objectives align, the seemingly impossible becomes possible. Human history is a testament to this. How could we have seen the success of John F. Kennedy's mission to land a man on the moon without a nation's whole-hearted support, or Germany's destruction of the Berlin Wall, or the elimination of apartheid in South Africa? Back in the day, these things were viewed as impossible dreams. They ran contrary to what generation after generation had accepted. However, once people bought into these ideas on a massive scale and common consent about their pursuit was achieved, nothing could stop them from being realized, not even legal structures that had been established long ago in order to try to prevent change.

On a smaller scale, the same is true for the Family Bank. Just as in a game of tug-of-war, a succession plan will be successful only if everyone affected is pulling in the same direction. When family members battle up front or behind closed doors, the game will most likely end with everyone in a morass of mud.

By developing a shared vision using the Family Bank approach, a family diminishes the likelihood for conflict. When all family members agree with what the larger family unit is aiming to achieve, individual expectations are managed. For instance, one priority of a family and its Family Bank may be post-secondary education for younger family members, in whatever form. If one Family Bank member earns a spot at an Ivy League university and another decides to pursue their passion at a trade school, neither sibling will be aggrieved by the different financial burdens their educational paths place upon the Family Bank. Through earlier Family Bank discussions, they will have learned a very important concept: that fair does not necessarily mean equal. They will understand that while the financial support required by one family member is greater than that needed by another, in this instance, the decision to support both is consistent with the family's shared vision.

Having a clearly articulated, shared vision is a foundational block of the Family Bank. It ensures that a family is working towards the attainable and attractive future they want for themselves, rather than a future prescribed by lawyers, accountants, and financial planners. Your plans for your family's future do not have to include buying more insurance or establishing a trust or a private charitable foundation. Any vision that addresses both the personal desires of your individual Family Bank members and your Family Bank's shared future will make your family members the architects of your own successful destiny.

## 4. Failures of Professionals

And speaking of the work done by professionals, 3 percent of succession plans failed due to their negligence. If it were possible, I would have this next point printed in big bold neon letters. It is:

> The commonly advised succession and wealth-transition structures, which are mostly established to minimize or defer taxes and control the next generation, result in failed

succession plans not because of the structures themselves, but in spite of them!

However, the bigger issue is that many families seeking advice on succession and wealth-transition planning are not the only ones unaware of this fact —so are their advisors. Unknowingly, many professionals in this subject area continue to recommend the products they are taught to use in their law schools or accounting and financial programs, for example, while not addressing the real reasons for failure. Is this not Albert Einstein's definition of insanity, "doing the same thing over and over again expecting different results"?

This is where the Family Bank comes in, a concept that turns the traditional approach to succession and wealth-transition planning upside down. As opposed to family members working together for the first time to overturn an estate's legal structure, such as a trust, families following the Family Bank approach are working together long before estate issues arise. Rather than beginning with lawyers and accountants, who are very good at what they do, and their commonly recommended structures, the Family Bank approach begins with the family itself. The Family Bank is built on a solid foundation of the family's shared values and vision, which is shared with the professionals as a reference framework for the services or products they provide. Once the family's assets have been assessed and prepared and the family has found a way to organize itself to reach its objectives, by establishing a governance structure, then, if agreed to by the Family Bank members, traditionally advised structures could be entered into.

# 2

# FAMILY BANK
# BASICS

I FIRST ENCOUNTERED the term "family bank" in James E. Hughes Jr.'s book *Family Wealth: Keeping it in the Family.* I liked the term right away. But that approach to succession and wealth-transition planning was not new to me, however. I had witnessed successful families following its core concepts over generations, though no name was formally given as to how they operated. The concepts of the Family Bank approach had simply become imbedded in the family's character.

Some of these families came to this method of succession and wealth-transition planning the same way I did: by experiencing a failed succession and wealth-transition plan from a ringside seat. Others were fed up with legal, accounting, and financial planning mumbo jumbo and were determined to find a simpler solution. Either way, we had all come to the same conclusion. The Family Bank approach makes far more sense than the generally accepted, professionally advised solutions that fail the majority of the time.

Like any sturdy structure, the Family Bank is built on a solid foundation. That foundation, strengthened through honest communication and trust, is created from the family's shared

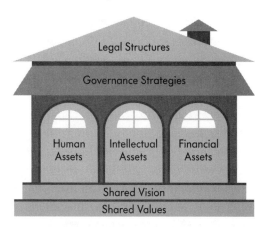

*Fig. 1: The Family Bank*

values and vision. And as I mentioned previously and illustrate above, the Family Bank is designed to be the custodian of all aspects of the family's wealth—not just the financial assets, but also its human and intellectual assets. Working together, Family Bank members devise strategies that will allow the family to realize its shared vision for all its forms of wealth and, as appropriate, the Family Bank serves as a prudent lender of those assets. Only then, and only if all the Family Bank members agree it is necessary, should professionally designed structures like trusts or foundations be investigated for their potential to assist the family in attaining its multigenerational goals.

The successful implementation of the Family Bank approach requires effective communication built on trust within the family and the preparation of all the Family Bank members to achieve their shared vision. The continuity of the Family Bank depends on each generation creating its own wealth while simultaneously serving as stewards of any inherited Family Bank assets. In today's flattening world, it is less likely that family businesses over multiple generations will remain identical to what was created by the first generation. In such cases, successful stewardship of the Family Bank's financial assets can include a reformatting of them. In my family of origin, my grandfather built a business by being one of the first to mass produce and can dog food; my mother and father reformatted their financial inheritance to build a successful and thriving communications, broadcasting, and professional sport organization; and my husband and I, both CAs and professional Investment Advisors, have reformatted our financial inheritance in the financial services and real estate industries.

First-generation family members who implement the Family Bank approach face some particular challenges. First of all, as initiators of this approach in the family, they are blazing a new trail. They are leading a process for which they have no previous training, experience, or expertise. Additionally, many families adopting the Family Bank approach are at a point in their family's life cycle where they are presided over by a dynamic first-generation wealth creator. These are individuals whose powerful dreams have inspired them to overcome significant odds to achieve full-blown financial success. Such human dynamos possess the innate qualities of personal strength, confidence, drive, determination, and thoughtful intelligence. In other words, when they first set out on their missions, they were blessed with a plentitude of human and intellectual capital but suffered from a scarcity of financial capital. Typically, these multitalented individuals have dedicated their lives to doing what they had to do in order to succeed. Often that has meant exercising absolute control over their organizations and the realization of their dreams. By definition, the Family Bank approach challenges that. The successful transition of a family's wealth from first generation to second generation will require the first generation to cede some control.

Ceding control is not easy for some. However, sharing control, rather than ownership, with the next generation at this stage is a pragmatic and proactive way to prepare the younger generation both for their future roles and responsibilities as Family Bank members and for successful independent lives. As we have seen, succession and wealth-transition plans fail 70 percent of the time. And traditional plans are dominated by legal structures intended to control the next generation. Equipped with this knowledge, Family Bank members must ask themselves which is preferable: working to develop Family Bank members who can successfully steward the Family Bank assets for future generations, or paying substantial fees to outside individuals for plans and structures that try to control the next generation and will likely fail.

An important part of the first generation's role is offering genuine respect and admiration to other Family Bank members, especially as their competencies and skills increase. Expressing your pride in younger generation members as they develop and mature gives them the cornerstone upon which self-esteem can be built. Self-esteem will provide the basis for each member to pursue fulfilling work and create a life independent of the family, realizing their own self-worth. Fully realized individuals on a path to pursuing their personal happiness will contribute strong, competent decision-making voices to the Family Bank.

Until a century ago, the word "wealth" was often used in connection with a family's health, spiritual life, even its type of employment. Today, we usually define wealth much more narrowly, simply as financial capital: the net cash left in bank accounts once all of the family's liabilities have been paid. This ignores the most important components of a family's wealth: what James E. Hughes Jr., in *Family Wealth,* calls its human and intellectual capital. The Family Bank approach reminds families seeking to sustain multigenerational transitions of wealth that the primary purpose of financial capital is as a tool to be used to nurture and strengthen each family member's human and intellectual capital, and thereby increase the assets of the family as a whole.

It is worth looking at each type of capital that makes up a family's wealth, to understand how the Family Bank can be used to increase them all:

## 1. Human Capital

The human capital of a family resides in the physical and emotional well-being of its individual members. Nurturing this human capital is of paramount importance to the Family Bank's success. If the individual family members are flourishing, then the family's most important assets are growing. If not, the Family Bank is weakened, and the likelihood of a successful generational transition is greatly diminished.

The Family Bank approach also recognizes the importance of each family member finding dignity and sense of purpose in life through their work. In addition, assisting each family member in finding the work that best enhances their pursuit of happiness is key. There is an overemphasis today on one's worth being based on what one earns. I cannot stress enough, however, that all work is of equal value to the growth of the family's human capital, regardless of its financial reward.

I once listened to a woman fervently argue that her legal career, with its charge-out rate of eight hundred dollars per hour, was more valuable to society than her nanny's job, with its charge-out rate of only twelve dollars per hour. I was outraged on many levels. Following her logic, the work of a professional athlete, who is paid $10 million per year to put a puck in the net or kick a ball between two goalposts, is more valuable than the work of a doctor at a children's hospital, who is paid considerably less. My point here? What a family member's job pays is no indication of the true value of that individual's work or worth to the family, to their Family Bank, or to society at large.

The emotional well-being of Family Bank members will be grounded in the values with which they are raised. And as the saying goes, the most important values in life are caught, not taught. These are the values that are lived out by parents in front of their children. In other words, what the children see is what the parents will get. The Family Bank approach encourages families to discuss their values, and makes this a cornerstone of the process.

## 2. Intellectual Capital

A family's intellectual capital can be defined as the sum total of everything each family member knows. No matter their life journey or aptitude, a family should stretch the intellectual scope of each member to achieve that member's own maximum level of learning. That way, each family member will contribute something unique to the wealth and strength of the family over the generations.

Even though I am a third-generation CA, and my husband is a CA, I have long since given up any idea of either of our sons following in our professional designation footsteps. A life spent trapped in the dreams of one's parents can be a nightmare. By contrast, a life spent pursuing one's personal dreams allows an individual to create a future of their own making. And in this rapidly changing world, I realize that the interests, ideas, and insights these two individual dreamers bring to our Family Bank is of more benefit to the whole family—to our joint intellectual capital—than the input of another CA might be.

## 3. Financial Capital

The financial assets of the Family Bank are the economic tools that will eventually be transitioned to the next generation of Family Bank members and the generations that follow. This is where the rubber hits the road. As a family discusses their Family Bank's financial assets in relation to the Family Bank's objectives—their shared vision—they must decide on the purpose of the family's financial capital. Is that purpose to buy toys for individual family members, or is the financial capital a tool to use to enhance the family's joint human and intellectual capital?

The gold standard is for each generation, as stewards, to leave the Family Bank, including the financial assets, even stronger than the one vouchsafed to them. This is an important concept for Family Bank members to understand. As stewards of the financial assets of the Family Bank, each generation is working for the human and intellectual benefit of future generations.

The Family Bank approach, as I have noted, is clear on this point. When a family sees its purpose as being to nurture and support each individual to find their individual calling, the family's human and intellectual capital increases. The irony is, of course, that increasing a family's human and intellectual capital also leads to the long-term preservation of the family's financial capital, and of the family as a whole. If a family focuses solely on maximizing its financial assets through tax-minimization strategies, rather than preparing the next generation as future leaders of the Family Bank, then they should not be surprised if members of the next generation become "Gucci loafers." There is nothing to stop a Family Bank member from pursuing a passion to rebuild collector cars, for example, as long as that passion is supported by the financial capital that member earned individually. In other words, by all means buy Gucci loafers and Prada pumps using money you expended the effort to earn. Those habits, however, should not be supported by the Family Bank.

The role of the Family Bank leaders will be critical in this regard. Part of the Family Bank process is engaging younger generations in financial conversations in an age-appropriate way. Young children pick up their attitudes towards money largely from watching the first generation in action, so at this stage being a role model is most important. By the time those children reach their late teens, though, it is a good idea to engage them in more detailed financial conversations. The Family Bank approach guides parents and grandparents in counteracting the message of our current free-spending culture. Through role modeling and open communication, Family Bank leaders can teach their children to be prudent stewards of the family's financial capital.

Here's an example drawn from my own life. The sale of my personal business triggered a financial windfall that would have permitted my husband and me to retire from our jobs at a young age and move our family to a tax-free tropical haven. However, since developing the human and intellectual capital of our young children—our most valuable family assets—is our priority, we recognized the critical importance of role modeling key values such as a strong work ethic, loyalty to our clients, passion for our work, and a commitment to self-sufficiency. As well, we recognized the need for us to be a wealth-creating generation ourselves, in order to sustain multigenerational wealth. We understood that there are no free rides. Knowing we had many earning years ahead of us, my husband and I made a values-based decision to undertake the stewardship of our Family Bank's financial assets rather than pursue a life of leisure.

IN THE PAST, parents often had greater ability to control their children. In a family business, for instance, succession was based on primogeniture, meaning the family business was automatically passed on to the first-born male. Daughters were counseled not to worry their pretty little heads about money issues. While times and views have changed on this issue, it is still common for many first-generation wealth creators to feel the need for control. Exercising control has defined their success in their business life, and sometimes this need for control spills over into their family lives. And when it comes to controlling the behavior of the younger generation, it might seem simplest to exert financial control through mechanisms like allowances or trust fund payments. Beguiling as these controlled handouts are to the younger generation, receiving them can lead to dependency and, from there, it is a slippery slope to entitlement. Rather, the Family Bank approach recognizes that there are exponential benefits to the Family Bank when all of its members pursue fulfilling, financially independent lives.

In addition, once the first generation of the family is gone, the siblings of the second generation will need to cooperate with one another. In succession planning lingo, the second generation is referred to as the "sibling partnership." The Family Bank approach recognizes this reality and works on the principle that the whole is greater than the sum of its parts. Working together can be a difficult task if the most influential role model the siblings had was a controlling parent. In such a situation, it is not surprising for each sibling to want to stretch their wings and be "the boss." Using the Family Bank approach, however, siblings learn how to compromise and work together.

In our Family Bank, my husband, our sons, and I work together as a team. We have agreed there will be common consent regarding the deployment of our Family Bank's financial capital. We openly talk through the pros and cons of specific financial decisions, encouraging everyone to share their unique ideas and perspectives. And as parents, my husband and I recognize that we do not actually "know everything," so we genuinely welcome the intelligent insights brought to our discussions by the next generation, our sons. As a result, these conversations have not only enriched the combined intellectual capital of our Family Bank, but they have also enhanced our sons' ability to cooperate with one another and helped shape their attitudes towards a future financial inheritance and its utilization, as they prepare to become heirs and stewards.

A great many families battle, and sometimes break apart, over real or perceived issues of fairness. Yet the succession and wealth-transition plans such families have designed and implemented, which strive to treat everyone equally in financial terms, are seldom fair. The Family Bank approach provides an excellent way to work around this potentially divisive issue. Families using this model understand that each family member has unique strengths and weaknesses. For that reason, each member will require a different level of support—emotional and financial—from the Family Bank.

Because Family Bank members agree on the family's long-term vision and the purpose of the Family Bank, decisions that may not be strictly *equal* among family members will still be seen as *fair*. Using the Family Bank approach means there are no secrets about how the family's assets will be deployed, and hence no need for behind-the-scenes maneuvering. The expectations of the next generation are managed as everyone learns what is expected of them and what kind of support they can expect from the Family Bank.

Another key element of the Family Bank approach is coming up with strategies for handling potential problems before they arise. In business terms, this is called having policies before need. Issues might arise, for instance, over who is allowed to be a member of the Family Bank. In earlier times, the Family Bank might well have included only the first-generation wealth creators and their children. However, the definition of "family" has changed dramatically over the last several decades. For one thing, the first-generation wealth creators are living much longer. That means first-generation asset owners may plan on skipping their own children, passing eventual ownership of the Family Bank's financial assets to their grandchildren instead. If such a plan is in accordance with the family's shared vision for the future, this scenario can be very successful.

Families today take on an array of shapes and sizes. Let's consider the Family Bank member who marries someone with children from a previous marriage. Will those children become members of the Family Bank? Or, what happens when a Family Bank marriage sours? Will the son- or daughter-in-law still be a Family Bank member after a divorce?

There are no right or wrong answers to these questions. Each family will decide such things for themselves. However, these are exactly the kinds of questions that should be considered long before the issues arise and become emotional. Policies of this nature, established well in advance, will go a long way toward easing possible family tensions about favoritism or fairness.

WHILE IT IS important to know what causes failure, it is also important to seek out and learn from success. History has provided us with spectacular family stories of successful succession and wealth transitions.

The famous Rothschild family, who at one time possessed the largest private fortune in the world, has successfully transitioned wealth over multiple generations, in part due to the use of a Family Bank concept. In the mid-eighteenth century, Mayer Amschel Rothschild established a business in Frankfurt dealing with coins and bills, a banking house, which he taught to his five sons. Recognizing the importance of the family's human and intellectual capital and the benefits of those capitals working together and learning from one another, he sent his five sons to five different European capitals to establish business operations with loans provided by their Family's Bank within the banking industry. At a time in history when news of the world was not readily available, he insisted that each son report back to him regularly about what they were learning, in general and related specifically to the marketplace in which they were operating. This resulted in the amalgamation of the family's intellectual capital and the strengthening of their human capital.

Mayer Amschel Rothschild is said to have been firm in passing down two specific guidelines. The first was that the family members were to work together, and the second was to be reasonable in their profit expectations. Mayer Amschel Rothschild recognized that their Family Bank would be stronger with the five brothers, with varying strengths and weaknesses, working together as opposed to independently of one another. As history unfolded, the successors to the five brothers also had varying degrees of competencies to continue running the Family's Bank, but working together allowed them to capitalize on their shared strengths and overcome individual weaknesses.

The Rothschild family motto is "Concordia, Integritas, Industria," which translates to "Harmony, Integrity, Industry." This family puts individual achievement and family unity first. To that end, the family has always held a gathering at which their shared values and vision are reaffirmed. So important is the gathering to their Family Bank that it has been noted that family members who fail to attend are locked out of their Family Bank. The rest is a matter of historical record. Through solid teamwork, good governance, shared family purpose, and the recirculation of the family's financial capital, the Rothschilds' personal Family Bank has successfully endured for more than two hundred years.

So, for those families who are quick to focus their tales on failed succession and wealth transitions in a friend's family, their community at large, or legendary historical examples—like the Vanderbilt family, who, as John Kenneth Galbraith noted, for several generations showed both the talent for acquiring money and the dispensing of it in unmatched volume—you should instead focus your energies on successful succession and wealth transitions. This is what the Family Bank approach does: it focuses on what the *successful* families do.

# 3

# YOUR FAMILY'S
# SHARED VALUES

S HARED FAMILY VALUES are a key foundational piece of the
Family Bank approach. A family's values define its view of
how the world works and how its members interact with each
other and other people. Ultimately, values guide family members in determining what is right or wrong, good or bad. Your
Family Bank will be built upon these values too.

When the members of a family articulate their values, they
find themselves answering questions like: What is important
to us? What are our priorities? What makes us special? Considerable research has been done on the subject of defining values,
and there are many how-to books on the topic. In fact, if you do
not know where to begin, I would recommend starting with an
internet search—you will find that there is a lot of information
available online. And then you will want to have a conversation
with your family members and list the values that are important to you. In the final analysis, you will come to realize that
your value system is unique to your family as it describes how
your family sees itself.

In the Family Bank model, conversations about the family's shared values provide an opportunity for strengthening

communication. In my experience, most families are comfortable discussing the issue of values, yet it is also a subject that can be easily overlooked. Family Bank leaders may assume that younger family members are receiving an education about values in the same way older members did when they were young. However, as many cultures have become more secular, and educators struggle just to keep students up on the three Rs— reading, writing and arithmetic—a values void has been created. And it is a void that mass media and children's peers have increasingly stepped in to fill.

The world has evolved in exciting and challenging ways from the time when the biggest influences on our children were their immediate family, their neighbors, their local school, and the three TV stations that rabbit ears pulled in. Those of us who remember those days find the current magnitude of information dissemination to be almost unimaginable. However, today's Family Bank leaders must stay abreast of (and often counteract) the various influences on younger family members, both in a general sense and when the younger people might be targeted. One of the best ways to do this is to schedule mutually respectful conversations across generations about shared family values. As a Family Bank leader, you will not only influence the values of the younger family members, but also help those members to appreciate why shared family values are so important.

One useful way to approach values-based conversations is to talk about role models—good ones and bad ones—encouraging family members to bring in examples from the workplace, school, the neighborhood, friends, extended family, and even media figures like celebrities or politicians. Clearly, there are an abundance of opportunities here. Taking time to explain the significance of a certain family value also demonstrates to the younger generation that you respect their experience and opinions.

The American writer James Baldwin once said, "Children have never been good at listening to their elders, but they have never failed to imitate them." It goes without saying that Family Bank leaders should role model the values they espouse. Otherwise, a family might find itself adding "hypocrisy" to its list of values.

As an example of a family-specific value, one that many first-generation wealth creators want to impress on the next generation is that of genuine caring and concern for the employees of the family business. In one family I know, the first generation is proud of the fact that their employees, while approached many times, never saw the need for a union, because the employees always knew they were a priority for the owners of the family business. In this instance, the subject came up in a family meeting I was facilitating, and it turned out the second generation was unaware of the significance of this value to the family business and the family. In every case where I have witnessed lived-out family values of this kind and they have been shared with younger family members, the next generation has embraced those values wholeheartedly. For one family, the value described here even became the driving idea for their family's shared values statement. Their list of values begins with: "We Care." All it took to establish that was an enlightening conversation regarding their family's shared values.

While every family's values are as unique as the family itself, there are several values shared by many families who have successfully transitioned all their forms of wealth over multiple generations.

## 1. Respect for the Luck Factor

Second-generation family members often directly witness the hard work, passion, determination, and single-minded focus required of Family Bank builders. Consequently, they appreciate and respect what it took for those builders to bring their dreams to life. However, these character traits alone are not enough—other entrepreneurs share these character traits but do not necessarily share the same financial success. Successful wealth creators recognize that, while certain traits are valuable, there is one element that is not within their control: luck. Luck comes in many forms, including good timing, being in the right place at the right time, and spotting an opportunity that might otherwise have been missed.

Successive generations need to understand this factor. They also need to ask themselves if they see the Family Bank as an inheritance or an heirloom.

An inheritance is different from a lottery win only in that it was expected. History has shown us time and again how quickly both inheritances and lottery winnings are lost due to foolish expenditures, inattention, incompetence, mismanagement, or other factors within the control of the inheritor or lottery winner. Unthinking, inheritors do not pause to consider what role luck has played in the accumulation of their family's financial assets. A financial inheritance may provide an opportunity only once every few generations for someone to strengthen not only their own human and intellectual capital but also that of successive generations.

The word "heirloom" has a much different resonance. However an heirloom comes into a family's hands, it is something to be taken care of and protected—and in the case of the Family Bank, to be stewarded so that future generations may share in the benefits. First-generation family members often took significant business risks to create the financial assets of the Family Bank. Going forward, Family Bank members should be encouraged to take reasoned financial risks with their own financial assets as well. But they should not take the same level of risk with the financial assets of the Family Bank. Once all family members understand that money does not grow on trees, they will appreciate that the financial assets of the Family Bank should be managed with a long-term view and in a more conservative and prudent manner.

## 2. Commitment to Stewardship

Stewardship is a concept that seems to have been lost in our instant-gratification culture. As defined in the *Merriam-Webster's* dictionary, stewardship is "the careful and responsible management of something entrusted to one's care." Spin doctors have politicians, environmentalists, and corporations use the word exhaustively, and their intent is clear: to convince the listener that these individuals or corporations are undertaking great responsibilities. I like to use the term in connection with the Family Bank: family members must see themselves as stewards of their family's wealth to ensure the Family Bank's sustainability.

By definition, the Family Bank is the custodian of a family's wealth: its human, intellectual, and financial assets. To nurture those assets over the long term, Family Bank leaders must make it a priority to develop members who are independent, self-fulfilled individuals, who are emotionally and physically healthy and well prepared for the future.

To be successful stewards of the family's financial assets, Family Bank members need to understand those financial assets must also support the human and intellectual assets of future generations. That means the financial assets of the Family Bank should be viewed as capital to be recirculated. This is a critical concept for a family to grasp as they work towards multigenerational wealth transitions. Like a traditional bank, the Family Bank may lend money to family members, but that money must be repaid. Without this provision, the family's financial assets will eventually be drained by financial outflows to an ever-increasing family base.

In preparing our sons for the concept of stewardship, it was important to draw their attention to the distinction between control and ownership. I had this specific conversation with one of our sons regarding a property that I legally own and he lives in while attending university. As he was preparing to take a semester off from university for a work opportunity, he commented that it was my decision about what should happen to the property, since I am the owner. I thanked him for his deference to my legal title, but I also made it clear that my ownership did not mean that I unilaterally controlled the property.

Technically speaking, my husband and I own all of our Family Bank's assets, but the four of us—as Family Bank members—share control equally. The decision on this property's place in our family's financial asset portfolio will be based on what is best for the entire family. At this stage, facilitating our son's education through the provision of stable accommodation, while investing in a fixed asset, is a better Family Bank decision than having him face unreliable accommodation term after term, along with the sunk cost of rent.

## 3. Strong Work Ethic

Work is essential for strengthening every class of asset in a family. Encouraging each family member to earn their own way in the world must be a top priority for Family Bank leaders. Whether or not the family could afford to cover each member's living needs and luxury expenses makes no difference. Work is a crucial element of any purposeful life. Mental health professionals tell us that we all need two things to be self-fulfilled: love and work. Research also shows that individuals who have built independent lives are able to communicate within their families in more meaningful and constructive ways.

For younger members of the Family Bank, work is the first step in cutting the umbilical cord. Adolescence is a critical time to experiment, and young people should be encouraged to enjoy journeys of self-discovery so that they can learn, and grow, from their inevitable mistakes. A job setback or an unsuccessful encounter with a difficult boss or client at this point in their lives is a learning moment, rather than the monumental disaster it could be once they are adults with their own family responsibilities and their career potentially on the line. Life experiences, reinforced by family conversations, strengthen a young adult's self-esteem, confidence, and belief in their ability to make it on their own.

By becoming self-sufficient through work, Family Bank members will develop the physical, emotional, intellectual, and financial capacity to lead lives entirely independent of the Family Bank. The chances for multigenerational survival of the Family Bank increase exponentially when its individual members feel free to add their earned opinions to the larger discussions. Now, that is the definition of freedom!

## 4. Open Communication About Money

As noted, for some families, money seems to be the last taboo topic. Those families using the Family Bank approach, however, recognize how vital it is to discuss the subject as a group. Failing to communicate openly about money can result in family members having a distorted idea about its availability and its place in a happy, productive life. Furthermore, as family members mature, countless chances to discuss the practical aspects of managing and investing money are missed. Precious opportunities are lost to inform growing children about the pitfalls and possibilities in managing one's financial affairs, and to discuss other examples of individuals and families who handle their money especially well or badly.

Barbara Hutton, the twentieth-century heiress, was quoted as saying, "I was glutted with privilege, softened by luxury, weakened by indulgent nannies—when you inherit as much money as I did, it destroys whatever incentive or goal you might have." When we read quotes like this, we should not find ourselves nodding our heads in agreement. We should be rolling our eyes, thinking, "Really? Money did all that? Where were her Family Bank leaders?"

### 5. Teamwork

Families following the Family Bank approach appreciate the fact that the family working together as a unit is more powerful than any one person can be working independently. As John L. Ward writes in *Perpetuating the Family Business: 50 Lessons Learned from Long-Lasting, Successful Families in Business*, the owners of a very successful family business in India were asked how the five very different siblings, all co-owners and co-CEOs, were able to work so well together. They said, "We see ourselves like the fingers on a hand. Some of us are taller and stronger than the others. Some of us are more dexterous. Some of us have more power. Some of us can't really do much without the others. Some of us are a little smaller and less able. But try to do anything without all five fingers and you quickly discover that each finger does make a contribution."

I am always inspired when I see a group of family members on sometimes quite divergent life paths pause to consider how fortunate they have been. While their individual personalities may be very different, what they have in common is a sense of shared values and an overwhelming pride in what the family has accomplished as a team. The Family Bank model allows each family member to feel they are part of something bigger and more important than themselves. This will drive the future vision of your family as a whole.

# 4

# YOUR FAMILY'S SHARED VISION STATEMENT

THE VISION a family creates for itself can energize not just current family members but members in many generations to come. Williams and Preisser used the word "mission" in their research into the reasons succession plans fail. In using the Family Bank approach, I prefer the word "vision." A mission statement implies that a target is set; when that target is reached, the mission is completed. A vision statement, on the other hand, is ongoing—it defines an entity's purpose vis-à-vis its values. With regards to your Family Bank, the vision is ongoing, dynamic and multigenerational.

Optimism is a personal philosophy of mine, and I encourage families to approach their shared vision statement in that way. Your shared family vision will not likely leap off the page at you. Depending on the ages and stages in life of your family members, and the existing level of conflict in your family, the process may take extensive consideration. A newlywed couple might arrive easily at a shared family vision statement. At the other end of the spectrum, in a multigenerational family that includes Family Bank leaders who are parents, grandparents, and maybe even great-grandparents, developing a shared family vision statement will take more time. Factors such as strained communication within the family, the greater number of people who must reach consensus, differing views on the purpose of the family, and the nature of the financial assets of the wealth-creating generations can all come into play. Preconceived expectations about the family and its financial assets can be particularly difficult to navigate.

However, there is no pressure to create the perfect shared family vision statement right away. You will begin by creating a draft. Like any succession and wealth-transition plan, your vision statement is not static, either; it must be flexible, able to bend and change as the world and your family both evolve. What will never change, though, is that your shared vision statement must be agreed to by all of your Family Bank members, biologically related or not, and must inspire them to action. In the end, no matter the stages in life of the Family Bank members, your shared family vision statement will posit a realistic, credible, and attractive future for the family.

Since a family's shared vision statement captures how the family wants to approach all of the Family Bank's assets—human, intellectual and financial, now and into the future—this statement is a logical extension of the family's shared values conversations. After all, a family's vision of itself in the future will reflect what is important to the family now. Remember that breakdown in communication tops Williams and Preisser's list of reasons why succession plans fail. By discussing shared values, Family Bank members strengthen their communication skills. Working together to create a vision that everyone agrees to and wants to strive for strengthens communication in the same way. The vision that is right for a family's future will be positive, uplifting, and inspiring for each Family Bank member.

A shared, clearly articulated family vision statement provides Family Bank members with the information they need to manage their individual expectations. It also sets a goalpost of sorts for the family. This is invaluable when it comes to evaluating the proposals put forward by the slick sellers of succession and wealth transition products. Using highly sophisticated focus groups, these hijackers dedicate themselves to muddling a family's vision and substituting a seemingly logical vision of their own.

Many of these "experts," for example, will advise families on the benefits of minimizing taxes or using trusts to control the next generation, without explaining the potential costs of these structures. As a CA and a personal business builder and seller, it would be scandalous of me to say that a family should ignore the tax consequences of a particular transaction, especially one of a significant size. Disregarding prudent tax advice along these lines could constitute a loss of family financial assets due to "inattention," as Williams and Preisser point out. However, a great deal of tax work today has crossed over into territory that has some very unpleasant consequences with regard to succession and wealth-transition planning.

The Family Bank approach treats the family like any high-achieving business. It realizes that the family must focus 70 to 80 percent of its efforts on developing of the asset side of its balance sheet, whether those assets are human, intellectual, or financial, and only 20 to 30 percent on the liability side. Taxes are a very short-term liability. Many professional advisors get this backwards, however, spending 70 to 80 percent of their time on the short-term liabilities of a family, like taxes, and leaving only 20 to 30 percent of their time to address the family's most important assets: its human and intellectual capital. To put it bluntly, a lot of time and money is wasted on professional fees to strengthen the family's financial assets—assets that will be frittered away by the following generations if they are unprepared.

The Family Bank approach specifically addresses the predominant reasons most succession plans fail. For example, an underlying priority of the Family Bank approach is establishing solid communication within the family. Many professional advisors, however, unaware that communication breakdown leads so often to the failure of succession and wealth-transition plans, often recommend complex tax-deferring or tax-minimizing structures, like trusts, that can complicate or even stifle family communication.

In a common scenario, individual family members often learn about their family's corporate and trust structure only at the time they file their first personal income tax returns. In signing their returns, they see that they are trustees, beneficiaries, preferred shareholders (of Class A, B, C, D, E, etc.), or common shareholders (of Class A, B, C, D, E, etc.) in an assortment of structures. They may wonder about the fact that money is moving between these entities under their name but not into their personal bank accounts. These young family members are seldom able, without preparation, to understand these complex structures or their roles and responsibilities in relation to them. The result is confusion about the family's expectations of them and what all these numbers and dollars really mean.

A young family member struggling to meet his monthly rent for shared accommodation, for example, may understandably feel resentment or anger towards older family members if he is unprepared for this new information regarding the flow and extent of financial capital. If this situation is left unaddressed, this resentful young person will mature into an adult who, unsurprisingly, will make decisions about the purpose of the family's financial assets that are at best uninformed and at worst completely misguided. What I have described is not something anyone wants for their family.

Communication is complicated enough in a family where we all wear a number of hats: daughter, sister, mother, aunt, etc. Adding complex functions like trustee, beneficiary, owner, employee, or shareholder into the mix, with no explanation about the roles and responsibilities, is a recipe for trouble. The traditional scenario of establishing structures that link roles to family members sets up perfect conditions for a breakdown in communication in the family and for all of the negative consequences that follow.

By following the Family Bank approach and clearly articulating a shared vision statement based on your family's shared values, you will not fall prey to the poor advice of a professional with a product to sell. In fact, as I have seen in my practice, a family's vision for its future is seldom focused on tax minimization or on controlling the Family Bank members. The Family Bank approach, with its emphasis on open and honest communication based on trust, allows each family to determine for itself what is important. That shared family vision will include preparing all family members to lead independent, self-fulfilled lives.

For instance, a shared vision statement, based on the family's shared values, may recognize the importance of a robust democratic political system, including a healthy tax system to provide infrastructure, education, healthcare, and other social safety nets. This family would inculcate in each generation the importance of exercising their vote. For this family, the solution to aggressive tax rates and wasteful government spending would be for Family Bank members to get out there and vote, get involved, work to change the politicians, or maybe even run for office themselves. Instead of using the financial assets of the Family Bank on the sunk costs of complex and confusing tax-planning strategies, this family might decide to invest its Family Bank assets in support of one member's political campaign running on a platform of much needed tax-spending accountability and reform. In other words, these Family Bank members may want to focus their efforts on changing the tax system rather than accepting the increasingly convoluted status quo. After all, someone's son or daughter has to be the prime minister or president.

A strong shared family vision statement links the past, present, and future, and invigorates Family Bank members by resonating with each person both emotionally and rationally. It should be relevant for the times, clearly outline the purpose and/or direction of the family, and reflect the family's special qualities. Emotional commitment depends on the shared family vision statement being deemed worthy by all Family Bank members.

Here's one example of how the emotional and rational components of a shared family vision fit together. My husband grew up in a small town with two brothers, a dedicated full-time mother, and a well-respected father. When my husband was in his early teens, he was crushed between two cars on his bicycle, which landed him in the hospital for over a month. If it had not been for Canada's universal healthcare system, his medical bills would have buried his parents, who were very financially responsible, in debt. However, because my husband's medical costs were covered by our tax-funded healthcare system, they managed to keep their financial heads above water. They went on to provide an education for each of their sons and also saved enough to invest some modest funds in raw land.

Decades later, my husband's parents are spending their retirement years turning this raw land into a productive commercial farm, which they own and operate. Because of the support of universal healthcare at a critical time and stage in their life, this family was able to maximize the development of all of the family's assets—human, intellectual, and financial—by providing opportunities for their sons to participate in programs that increased their physical, emotional, and intellectual capabilities, as opposed to the entire family being buried by an insurmountable mountain of medical bills. Today, all of the family members, including my husband's parents in retirement, are independent, productive members of society. As a family, they have paid far more back into the tax system that supports universal healthcare than they ever utilized after my husband's accident.

On the rational front, looking out over the next few decades, our governments are warning us that our personal debt levels are too high. Compounding the problem is the fact that many of us have grown accustomed to our entitlements. Yes, I said entitlements. The term does not apply only to those who I call cookie-jar kids (more on them later). It applies to all of us who assume that government will always be in a position to finance, in full or in part, our education system, healthcare, and other social safety nets.

Our governments have not been prudent financial stewards of the money we pay through taxes. Like many citizens, they have spent more than they have taken in and this reckless overspending cannot go on forever. This is one of the ongoing conversations my family has at the dinner table. Because our sons understand the important role universal healthcare has played in their family's history, and because they realize they may face a future in which they are required to pay for these kind of entitlements that are currently funded by our government, they readily agree that providing for the health of future generations of our family is a worthy purpose of our Family Bank. Based on our shared values, this purpose is reflected in our family's shared vision statement.

Your family's vision will motivate commitment when it provides purpose and meaning to individual family members' lives and to the family as a whole, so don't hesitate to be bold in creating your vision statement. A shared vision statement reaches much further than minimizing or deferring taxes, or attempting to permanently control all the assets of the family. Big dreams can be achieved—a family just has to be inspired to reach for them. Different cultures have imbedded in them differing views around succession and wealth-transition planning. Who knows, you may find that something new to your family's vision for the future may be widely accepted in another part of the world.

A respected friend and client of European descent, who grew up in a home where he witnessed successful succession and wealth transitions over multiple generations firsthand, one day commented to me, "Big dream, it can't be done here!"

"Excellent," I thought, "a challenge!" You see, after this client had spent decades of dedication and hard work creating a significant nest egg of human, intellectual, and financial assets, accountants and lawyers had had their way with him. Consequently, his family corporate and trust structure was very complex. In fact, he had initially contacted me to discuss the idea of establishing another trust structure. After reviewing his family's existing structure of trusts and corporations, I asked him what he wanted to achieve at the 30,000-foot level. In other words, what did he want for the future of his family? He paused before answering and I swear I could have heard a pin drop. Finally, he looked at me wide-eyed and said, "You know, no one has ever asked me that."

I was stunned. This client had spent lots of time and money on professional advisors yet not one of them had ever bothered to ask him what his vision was for his family, let alone what role the other family members played in that vision.

After further consultation, an additional trust structure was added—but only after a clear purpose for adding another trust, which had nothing whatsoever to do with tax deferment or control, was articulated, and it was determined that the advantages of this structure outweighed its potential disadvantages. Interestingly, though, our meetings and ongoing discussion started another conversation, in the family. In this case, the client's children are in their sixties and his grandchildren are in their twenties. The Family Bank approach is an idea the family is weighing as it considers skipping a generation with its future wealth transition.

A successful shared family vision statement requires input from all family members who have earned or are working on earning a voice in the Family Bank, regardless of their age. That means listening carefully to others. As my husband quite rightly pointed out to me, humans have two ears, two eyes, and one mouth. I understand his point. Active listening is an essential aspect of effective communication. All Family Bank members must genuinely feel their voices count in the articulation of a shared family vision statement. When everyone knows their ideas have been thoughtfully considered, there is a real sense of fairness in the process. The result is a vision statement with a far greater likelihood of general acceptance.

Finally, when discussing your family's shared vision, encourage young family members to think outside the box, and think for themselves. The question *why* should be encouraged. Young Family Bank members with the confidence to ask questions and seek answers are building the skill set needed for strong decision-making. Look for ways to help them develop their communication skills, both written and oral. A good leader is always a good communicator, someone who can communicate their ideas and visions to others so that they are easily understood. The Family Bank approach provides many opportunities for all members to practise their communication skills in a friendly, non-critical environment. These skills not only prepare them as future leaders of the Family Bank but also strengthen their confidence in their own ability to present themselves as they mature and head into long-term relationships and seek independent work.

You will know that you have articulated the right vision statement for your family when all Family Bank members agree with it and are excited by it. If Family Bank members are openly conflicted or, worse, are talking and stirring up trouble behind each other's backs, you will know that the process is not yet complete.

One family I work with created the following vision statement: "To always be able to gather in genuine fondness with one another at the dinner table." Their statement is brilliant, and it suits them to a tee. My first meeting with the Family Bank leaders was at their home. Like them, their home is warm, friendly, and inviting. As we walked through the dining room, I noticed that a number of tables had been pushed together end to end running from the dining room into the living room. Mismatched tablecloths under clear plastic and an assortment of chairs made the table one long inviting unit. It did not take a lot of conversation to learn that this was the family's gathering place. It was around this long table, my clients told me, that the family communicated regularly, nurturing members of all the generations in an open and honest way to prepare everyone for what to expect in the future. This family had already established the fundamentals of a Family Bank: communication and shared values. Crafting a shared vision statement was the next logical step.

You might now be looking for more examples; it is what I did when I first studied this topic. Interestingly, over the years I have gathered together quite a list of examples, but I have long since put it aside. This is because there is more learned from the process of communicating and working together to create a shared family vision statement that captures your unique family based on your previously defined values than from following or adopting someone else's. The strength of the shared family vision statement that will set the destiny for your Family Bank will be exponentially more powerful when, through ongoing communication built on trust within the family, it is created by the well-prepared Family Bank members themselves.

# 5

## YOUR FAMILY'S HUMAN AND INTELLECTUAL ASSETS:
### Preparing the Next Generation

ONCE YOU have arrived at the point where your family has a good idea of your shared values, and you have had some fun together creating an appealing, meaningful, and realistic shared vision for the future, the next step is to start making that vision a reality. The question Family Bank leaders need to ask is this: do our Family Bank members have what it will take to get the job done for years to come? If not, what do we need to do to get there? It can be a humbling experience to see ourselves for who we are, rather than who we pretend we are, but it is an essential part of the Family Bank process.

Over time, a successful family honestly assesses and reassesses itself, building on its strengths and working on its weaknesses. Research shows that although people's values are largely set by the age of twenty-five, their individual competencies and capabilities will evolve as they continue to learn and develop. This will be true in your family as well. As a result, your initial appraisal will involve not only evaluating the human and intellectual assets of your Family Bank but also the planning required to ready Family Bank members with the skills, aptitudes, and attitudes necessary to make your family's shared vision a reality. If you have members who are not currently prepared for ownership, like young children, your plans will likely include trusted legal guardians who share your family's values, understand the vision you have for your Family Bank, and can be relied upon to prepare these minors for future ownership.

In the initial stages, one or more Family Bank leaders will be overseeing this assessment process. Typically, the first Family Bank leader is whoever technically owns the financial assets and is thinking about how best to transition them to the next generation. This might be one spouse or both. Whatever the case, those assuming leadership will be agents for change in the family. By definition, a leader has followers, and effective leaders also have the respect of those followers. Actions that help earn this respect include being a good listener and consistently role modeling the family's shared values. The Family Bank leader should be someone the other members are proud of and willing to learn from as they prepare themselves for their eventual ownership of the Family Bank.

Education is necessary for building strong intellectual assets in your Family Bank. First of all, the pursuit of an education instills self-discipline, and the wonderful thing about self-discipline is that it can be applied to everything in a Family Bank member's life. Some other benefits of education to the Family Bank include members having the ability to track elaborate thought processes and develop imaginative concepts. Education fosters creativity. Also, gaining an education will remind each Family Bank member for the rest of their lives that they possess the intelligence, tenacity, and grit to pursue whatever achievement they aspire to, including reaching their family's shared vision.

It is important to note that I am not referring here only to degrees from the finest business schools, or even to a university education. Your Family Bank will benefit the most from each member pursuing an educational goal that is meaningful to them and challenges them to their greatest capacity. Education is not only about the specific knowledge that is acquired, but also about the process of earning it. It is this process that will be a part of each family member earning, no matter the vocation, a respected voice in the Family Bank. Reaching one's individual potential requires character traits such as commitment, hard work, high standards, and expertise. All of these attributes lead to excellence—excellence that in turn will contribute to your Family Bank.

The best Family Bank leaders will themselves be continual learners: curious, optimistic, and excited by the challenges presented in a world that, like the colors in a kaleidoscope, is constantly changing. In fact, a love of learning is not an option for a successful Family Bank leader. It is a necessity. One of my sons, currently a university student in engineering and computing science, has on numerous occasions shared Moore's Law with our family. Moore's Law, as proposed by Intel cofounder Gordon Moore in 1965, stated that the processing powers of computers would double every two years. Moore's peers laughed at him. But where are we today? Computer processing power is now doubling every eighteen months.

Nothing remains the same for very long anymore. Consequently, what appears to be the right vision for your family's future self will change more frequently than it would have ever before in human history. Those families who do not keep up will find their visions quickly becoming obsolete. They will miss opportunities to create bolder, brighter, and more relevant visions for their future. Ongoing learning, in addition to the insights of each generation of Family Bank members, will keep Family Bank leaders abreast of these changes. Leaders who exhibit a continual love of learning—and the self-discipline that this requires—are powerful role models for younger family members who will eventually become the leaders of the Family Bank themselves.

There is another kind of learning that will be essential in the stewardship of your Family Bank's financial assets. Every Family Bank member, young or old, must keep up with the financial realities of the twenty-first century. I am pleased every time I open a newspaper, a journal, or a publication from a professional financial organization to discover an article on money matters. However, it is important to begin educating family members about these matters at a young age, in an age-appropriate manner. As evidenced by the currently soaring rates of personal debt, many people appear to be getting this kind of information too late, long after poor financial habits have become entrenched. With such articles published in the financial section of a newspaper, for example, I also wonder if the excellent advice is really reaching the people who are in greatest need of this guidance, or if it is being read predominantly by financial professionals like me. There are likely many people who either scan the financial section superficially, getting lost in all the complicated jargon, or routinely toss it aside, like I do with the driving section.

These financial advice articles are generally very good. Commonly, they argue that people should divide up their earnings and place the money in different accounts to cover savings, emergency funds, retirement, and the like. This is sound advice. But in our immediate-gratification, product-pushing culture, dominated by slick advertisers, it is very difficult for most of us to sustain such a level of self-control. That's particularly true if we have not learned personal money management skills from childhood on and have no understanding of why this kind of discipline is so important for our future.

There is another point I want to make here, too. As a nation, we are constantly warned that our personal debt levels are too high. Well, here is a news flash: our governments have not been prudent financial stewards of the money we pay to them through our taxes. Like individual citizens, governments have also been spending more than they take in, and it is a situation that cannot go on forever. As noted earlier, this is a conversation all Family Bank members need to have, since social safety nets, including government-funded pension plans, will be affected in the future.

Remember, the most compelling shared vision for your family will be one that makes both emotional sense and rational sense. Pension plans are actually a terrific subject for a Family Bank conversation. Pensions are something we hear a lot about, but very few of us really understand them. Many young people might have heard somewhere along the way that the government provides a pension to Canadians over the age of sixty-five. However, they may have no idea about whether this pension plan is overfunded or underfunded and what that all means. We often hear about workers going on strike in different government-funded sectors. Often the primary reason given for this labor unrest, at least in the media, is wages. Even as the debate rages and kids are kept home from closed government-funded schools, the media coverage seldom mentions the pension benefits, the future income during retirement, this segment of the labor force is contractually entitled to. All of these are important issues every Family Bank member should be clear on as they begin working towards their own financial independence. If Family Bank members are made aware that, in the future, they may be required to pay privately for pension entitlements currently funded by government, they may be more willing to place their money in their savings and investment accounts early on.

Younger Family Bank members also need to be educated about the profound changes in our banking system. As a young girl, I often went to our local bank with my mother, where she would withdraw a set amount of cash each Friday for household expenses like food and gas. The bank tellers and branch manager had built long careers at the bank, and over time we developed real relationships with them, based on their genuine caring and concern for each member of our family. We respected the bank's employees and saw them as custodians, safe keepers of our family's cash balances and prudent lenders when additional money was required, pure and simple.

Then something happened: banks expanded their product offerings and a sales culture appeared. From the bank's perspective, and that of their shareholders, it was a brilliant idea. Today, with a click of a computer button, banks have insider knowledge of their clients' financial affairs. This knowledge itself is not the problem; the problem is what banks have done with this information. Almost overnight, bankers were apparently experts in a multitude of industries, including insurance, investments, and trusts. For my mother, who is now in her nineties and at a stage in life where genuine, trusted relationships are perhaps more important than ever before, this development has been distressing and disappointing—her personal relationship with the bank has been severed. What used to be a service culture has been replaced by a sales culture, and the bank's employees do not see a future in which she, a woman in her nineties, will buy any of their other products. Many people find themselves in similar situations.

How does this product-pushing and cross-selling at the bank work? Here is one example. A close friend of mine downsized her home, and the result was a nest egg of capital that she earmarked for her retirement. On one of her visits to her bank, a teller noticed the lump-sum savings in my friend's account. Caught unaware by this well-spoken, likeable young teller, my friend was introduced to an on-site seller who talked her into buying one of the bank's mutual fund products. This is not the way to make a prudent investment decision, and my friend was unknowing about what was going on behind the scenes. She was not made aware of the fees that might be involved with this kind of product, either imbedded in the product or up front. Nor did she realize that the teller was likely incentivized, through anything from bonus pay to performance review recognition, to refer my friend to this licensed on-site "advisor."

Another big change in the banking industry relates to credit. When I was young, I recall my mother having a credit card with the local gas station. She could buy only gas with it, not gas and a latte. Furthermore, the credit card had only been extended to my mother and father because they had an established flow of income through solid employment.

Later on, banks saw an opportunity to make more money by entering the credit card business. They are now quick to provide us with credit cards to buy the things that peers, advertisers, and professionals tell us we need. You see, they make substantial income on the usurious nature of this arm of their business. (Usury is the practice of lending money at unreasonably high rates of interest.) Many people do not pay off their balances every month, which means the interest charges mount. Suddenly, that expensive latte just got a whole lot more expensive.

Banks strategically target certain demographic groups in our society to sign up for their credit cards. One of the groups is university students. These students typically have not yet established a solid employment record. Even so, the banks have been known to offer inducements for them to sign up, including new laptop computers and cell phones. "But why?" you ask. "How could students meet the definition of good credit risk?" The answer is that this demographic has a fair share of young people from affluent homes. Parents may tell their children that any credit card debt belongs to them. However, once cards are maxed out, parents often pay the debt off in the end, high interest charges and all, not wanting the child to enter adulthood with a bad credit rating.

Corporations and advertisers go to great lengths to convince us to buy what they are selling. In my business, I see an endless number of cases in which people have received financial advice that is at best questionable. Think about it: every time we turn on the radio, surf the internet, or open a newspaper, we encounter yet another advertisement for some slickly packaged financial industry product described in emotive terms. The better ads even employ a little wit, for more appeal.

Here is a radio advertisement I awoke to at 4:30 one morning. A national lending company was aggressively advertising that if you own your own home, you could get a loan from them with no questions asked. The advertisement featured a short conversation between a potential borrower and a representative from the lender, along the following lines:

Borrower: "For an addition to my home?"
Lender: "You own your home?"
Borrower: "Yes."
Lender: "Approved!"
Borrower: "To expand my business?"
Lender: "Approved!"
Borrower: "To establish a sasquatch farm ..." (pause for dramatic effect) "... with a tennis court, of course."
Lender: "Of course ... Approved!"

I do have a sense of humor, and I understand advertisers' efforts to have a little fun with a subject that can, for some people, be mind-numbingly dull. However, the unsophisticated listener will not notice that some vital information is missing from this advertisement, like the fact that you may be putting your home at risk if the expansion of your business fails and you are unable to pay off this easily acquired loan. That is not to mention what will happen to your ability to pay off the loan when interest rates rise from current record-low levels.

No one pays for costly, extensive marketing unless they have something to gain. Today, as we are inundated with a plethora of advertising campaigns and other dubious sources of financial information, we should evaluate these claims with three questions in mind: "What does this pocket-picker paying for the advertising want me to purchase?" Then: "What is the downside risk to me if I purchase what is being sold?" And then, for entertainment's sake: "What is the advertiser using/saying/ singing to try and hook me?"

I had fun using similar questions as a game with my children when they were young. By encouraging them to think independently about and thoughtfully question the sources and intent of media-supplied information, I was preparing them for the future onslaught of all things marketed and advertised. As one example, at a young age, my sons would sometimes get it into their heads that they needed the sugary food products advertised in the commercial breaks between their favorite cartoons. The questions in the game we played became a terrific tool for showing them what was really going on. As young men, they are now bombarded with advertisements for financial products, and they realize they are being marketed to. The only real difference between the sugary food products and the financial products is that one rots your teeth and the other your financial security.

Part of assessing your family honestly is examining members' attitudes about lifestyle and work. I raised this issue in Chapter 3, when discussing the importance of shared values. It is worth revisiting, however, since many Family Bank leaders do not realize that they must specifically address their own legacy lifestyles or else inadvertently create what I call cookie- jar kids.

You might think the term "legacy lifestyle" refers to the kind of lifestyle in which I was raised. My family skied through the winters at a world-class resort where we owned a chalet and where, when the lift lines were too long at the bottom of the mountain, our parents had me and my siblings helicoptered to the top. When summer arrived, we jetted to the family yacht in the Mediterranean. We spent sunshine-filled days on the beaches of Saint-Tropez and mellow evenings in the bars and restaurants under the shadow of the royal palace in Monaco. Yes, this is an example of a legacy lifestyle, but there are, of course, other experiences that could certainly apply. A legacy lifestyle, as I define it, is one in which an individual enjoys a quality of life based on a certain level of affluence earned by another individual. Affluence is a relative term, meaning different things to different people, but it can be measured by looking at a family's non-essential expenditures. For one family, affluence may mean owning a small speedboat, and for another, it could mean owning a fully crewed yacht.

Whatever a family's lifestyle, the role the Family Bank plays in paying for it must be made clear to younger family members. Otherwise, children may grow up simply assuming that when they are adults, their lifestyle will remain the same. This assumption may lead to nasty entitlement issues. Holding regular ongoing conversations with all family members about the purpose of the Family Bank can prevent some of these legacy lifestyle children from facing a rude awakening when they realize in early adulthood that the effort, talent, abilities, or correlated earnings required to sustain such a lifestyle are no longer within their reach.

For children whose families do not have surplus financial capital, there is simply no metaphorical cookie-jar available. Consequently, by late adolescence, these children are applying for their first jobs. Job seeking and employment are vital components of maturation for all young people. It teaches them, perhaps for the first time, the effort it takes to earn their own money, as well as the true value of a dollar. However, the parents of cookie-jar kids often do not treat the ability for their child to earn their own living as a priority. After all, children who hang out all summer at the cottage lose the opportunity to pursue independent work.

These adolescents quickly learn that the cookie jar is full and the lid is easy to loosen. While their parents enjoy dockside relaxation at the cottage by day and party the nights away, these children are watching and learning. So, when the ski boat needs gas, or a teenager wants new board shorts, skate shoes, and some beer for that night's party at a buddy's cottage, no problem. These kids simply reach into the cookie jar. As these children mature, however, the postponing of their independence, including financial independence through work, is anything but a sensible idea. True happiness is realized through the ability to lead a free life, not only physically but also emotionally and financially. A cookie-jar kid, by definition, is not free; he or she is dependent on the parental supply of cookies in the cookie jar.

I believe that true financial happiness can only be found when you fill your own cookie jar with cookies you have baked yourself. Using the Family Bank approach, every family member will be prepared and assessed to ensure that they are on the path to becoming independent self-fulfilled individuals, eventually baking their own cookies—and maybe even running their own bakery. This is when the most important assets of the Family Bank, the human assets, are their strongest and healthiest.

Now consider the cookie-jar kid who becomes a cookie-jar adult. His parents may feel sorry for him, because he is apparently unemployable, but the reality is that the cookie-jar adult refuses to accept employment that he considers to be below his natural station in life. I have witnessed cookie-jar adults resorting to emotional blackmail when their elderly parents attempted to glue shut the lid of the cookie jar. They could also be individuals who assume that because one Family Bank member was assisted in some way, perhaps with a loan to buy a car, they must receive an equal benefit. They have lost sight of the fact that fair and equal are not the same thing. When the Family Bank approach is used, these kinds of issues are less likely to arise. As part of the process, everyone agrees to the purpose of the Family Bank and the deployment of its assets.

If the goal of the Family Bank is for every member to lead a free and independent life, finding paid work will be a priority. Therefore, the Family Bank would likely approve a reasonable car loan to assist a member in reaching their place of employment if there were no other reasonable means available. If another member wanted a car loan simply to travel back and forth from the shopping mall with their friends, though, that would not even be up for discussion. The request would not align with the family's priorities for their Family Bank.

By definition, the Family Bank approach is a team activity. Although someone must take the very important lead role to begin with, in a short period of time the Family Bank will involve a group of individuals working together. Articulating the family's shared values and vision requires robust conversations among people who are willing and able to work together. Additionally, the Family Bank approach makes a clear distinction between ownership and control. Once members have earned a voice on the Family Bank board, they become voting members in the stewarding and deployment of Family Bank assets. This is one of the profound benefits of the Family Bank approach. By working together, Family Bank members can amass decades of experience in preparing for the eventual transition of ownership, bypassing the need for the "beyond the grave" control structures typically recommended by succession and wealth-transition advisors. Over time, the Family Bank leaders will be continually assessing the family's ability to work together effectively and can suggest adjustments as necessary.

In my family, we operate intentionally as a team to prepare our children for their future roles as stewards of our Family Bank. And working together over time allows our sons, who spent their growing-up years competing with each other, as all siblings do, to learn to work together in an adult sibling partnership with a shared purpose. Working together as a team allows our sons to see each other as the adults they have become rather than as the children they once were.

On more than one occasion, I have been asked by a client what to do when there is one Family Bank member who is not, for lack of a better phrase, willing to play nice. Forcing a relationship is never a good idea, and it is counterproductive to the Family Bank's shared desire to work together for a brighter future for the family. So I always offer the same response, employing a little humor to brighten things up: "Then you should consider pruning the family tree."

This advice may sound harsh. However, it is of no value for the family to wait for someone who does not want to be there, or who has perhaps joined another family by now. Remember, we are talking about the Family Bank here, not the family itself. Someone unwilling to do what it takes to earn a voice in the Family Bank can still be welcome at a family dinner. In fact, keeping the door open is always a good idea. Time itself has a way of changing an individual or group perspective on the past and keeping everyone in the loop may have unexpected results.

In one situation I encountered, one family member was not remotely interested in the Family Bank; specifically, in its financial assets or the family business operations. This person had fallen on hard times and chose to live on the streets. As time passed, this family formalized their philanthropic work by establishing a private foundation. When the disenfranchised family member learned of this development, it resonated with him. A short while later, he managed to pull his life together. The process of turning his life around earned him the respect of the other Family Bank members, as he demonstrated tenacity, purposefulness, hard work, and the ability to change. The man was welcomed back into the Family Bank and later assumed an active role in the family's philanthropic foundation.

Stage in life is another important factor to consider when assessing individual Family Bank members. A young child will not likely have a direct voice in the Family Bank, but they will learn from role modeling and from listening to conversations about the family's shared values and vision. By adolescence, this individual will have developed a clearer understanding of the family's shared values and vision. Once this family member reaches young adulthood, they can choose whether or not they want to earn a voice on the Family Bank board.

For families adopting the Family Bank approach later in life, with family members who are already adults, it is advisable to start slowly. While assessing the strengths and weaknesses of Family Bank members is still necessary, it is wise to allow some leeway for those who are already overloaded in their personal lives. Involvement in the Family Bank is ongoing, but the level of commitment must accommodate each Family Bank member's stage in life. For instance, a college-age child may not seem interested in the Family Bank. This is normal; people that age are often focused on finishing their education, finding a job, and becoming financially self-sufficient. They might be striving for separation from their family as they struggle for independence. Another example is the young adult who has a new career, a young marriage, and maybe even young children, who understandably may not have the time to participate fully in Family Bank conversations with the rest of their family.

Individuals pursuing lives independent of their families, including in financial terms, are actually developing strong human and intellectual assets for the Family Bank, even if they currently are not able to be directly involved. Again, it is strongly advisable to keep these family members in the loop. When communication is circulated regarding the Family Bank, include them on the distribution list. This can maintain or even improve trust within the family, since everyone is receiving the same information and has the same opportunities to learn about how the Family Bank operates. When it comes to communication within families, more is always better than less. An inclusive approach will prepare individual family members for their future roles and responsibilities and discourage the growth of behind-the-back rumor mills.

One of the advantages of the Family Bank approach is that it takes a long-term view, which means that you and your family members have time to nurture and further develop the human and intellectual assets of the Family Bank members going forward. For any member willing to share in their Family Bank's vision, opportunities for active learning and preparation for the successful future generational transition of the Family Bank lie ahead.

# 6

# ASSESSING YOUR FAMILY'S FINANCIAL ASSETS

As you will know from reading this far, your family's shared vision will be your priority when assessing the purpose and role of your family's financial assets. If you stand back far enough, everything is in the numbers. The first time I heard that line was from my professor of statistical analysis at university. I was young and eager to learn, and I hung on his every word. And that phrase has never left me. However, as I went on to earn designations as a CA and as an Investment Advisor over the years, my understanding of it deepened. I know today that while the numbers are very important, and must be wisely heeded, it is by considering the entire forest—the family's human, intellectual, and financial assets—that you will make the best decisions regarding the stewarding of the trees. The Family Bank approach considers the vision your family has of its future, and the roles and responsibilities each Family Bank member will have to assume to make that shared vision a reality, in conjunction with the deployment of your family's financial assets.

For families who use the Family Bank approach, money is not a taboo topic. In fact, the opposite is true. Money education is as essential to a mature adulthood as sex education is. The more knowledgeable Family Bank members are about the family's financial assets, the more successful the process will be. This kind of information becomes part of ongoing communication within the family. On an age-appropriate basis, Family Bank members should be made aware of the family finances, as this will educate them also as to how the family is able to afford its lifestyle. This information will be invaluable to the next generation as they look to their own futures, including careers, and determine what lifestyle they can reasonably expect. And as children grow older, they can be specifically included in conversations about how best to deploy the financial assets of the family. Again, using the Family Bank approach, these decisions will be based on the family's shared values and vision. Encouraging Family Bank members to participate in financial discussions allows them to take pride in the stewardship of the family's assets and prepares them for future responsibilities.

The size and scope of the Family Bank will depend on the form those financial assets take. In my family, the sale of a significant family business triggered liquid financial assets for our Family Bank, so our initial stewardship decisions ran more to passive investments: financial markets, real estate, and collectibles. Other Family Banks will have financial assets of a more active nature—for example, an operating family business. The tools necessary to administer your Family Bank's financial assets may vary from passive to active, but the role and responsibility of generational stewardship does not.

There is lots of excellent information out there, in book form and available through the wise counsel of business people in your community, for those interested only in succession planning for the family business. The specifics of that subject are beyond the scope of this book. However, since I have had substantial experience with family businesses, I know there are a couple of questions you should ask yourself long before drafting a detailed family business succession plan.

First of all: "Is it the dream of the next generation to continue the family business?" Aspirations are highly individual and unique. Although some parents may try, no one can ever do the dreaming for someone else. The succession of a family business to the next generation has to be the dream of those next-generation members, not only that of the current owners. Passion should never be underestimated as a requirement for success in business.

Not long ago, I attended a wine-tasting dinner hosted by John Skinner, the owner of Painted Rock Estate Winery. John retired at a young age from his first career to pursue his dream of owning and building, from the foundation up, an estate winery in the interior of British Columbia. In our brief initial conversation, I was impressed by John's passion for his business. His wines have won multiple awards and John had just returned from a very productive trip to cement his winery's long-term relationship with North American Premiere Wine Shop in China. This wine aficionado's positive energy and excitement were palpable. What further caught my attention was that his dream is alive and thriving. As the company's visionary, John Skinner is the force behind the business. Having a powerful dream is a universal characteristic for successful entrepreneurs.

In his essay "A Reflection on Modern Psychology and the Question of Family Relationships," James E. Hughes Jr. emphasizes the power of a dream by posing a series of questions. First, he asks: of the roughly 7 billion people living on this earth, how many can remember even one of their dreams from the night before? The answer is very few. His second question is, how many of those people can remember that dream three days later? The number significantly diminishes. Next, how many of those dreams remain in the person's conscious mind and evolve into an idea? Hughes says the number of evolutionary dreams is an insignificant, minimal number. Of those that do, though, how many become material for a viable enterprise? According to Hughes, the number would be akin to a drop of water in the ocean. Finally, of those dreams that do materialize, how many result in something like John Skinner's company, which was named the top winery in B.C. and number three in Canada at the *Wine Access* Canadian Wine Awards within just three short years? The number is so tiny that it is statistically impossible.

I have personal experience with the power of a seemingly unattainable dream. I know what it is like to passionately pursue a vision long after others would have given up. The power of the dream my brother Arthur and I shared resulted in our shared ownership and, along with our partners, John and Bruce McCaw, purchase of a National Hockey League franchise, the Vancouver Canucks; and the purchase of a National Basketball Association franchise, the Vancouver Grizzlies, one of the first two NBA franchises awarded to Canadian cities; and construction and private financing of Vancouver's GM Place (now Rogers Arena).

Giving back to the community was one of the many values role modeled for my siblings and me by both of our parents. My mother and father viewed our family's 1974 acquisition of the controlling interest in the Vancouver Canucks franchise as a way of giving back to our community. At that time, other potential buyers had been approached, but none were interested in a business that was not profitable. My parents, however, recognized the importance of this professional sports franchise to its fans and the city over the dark and dreary west coast winters.

I am the youngest member of our family. Our parents raised my siblings and me with a profound sense of what it meant to represent the ownership of a professional "community" sports franchise. They taught us that we owed a duty of care to all members of the hockey operation—players, management, and support staff—and had a responsibility to do our best to provide a sustainable, winning franchise for Vancouver fans. My family lived and breathed hockey. Our commitment to the team was so strong that quite often the team's on-ice performance affected the moods of family members. When the team won, we were jubilant. A loss was another matter, and the Canucks lost a lot of games in those days.

As owners, my family and I were obligated to demonstrate our support for the team. (My husband Paul, then my boyfriend, made quite a first impression on my family by cheering exuberantly for the opposing team from the family box.) We made every effort never to miss a game. During the hockey season, we spent weekends at our winter home at a ski resort a good two-hour drive from the arena. In those days, the highway was dark and treacherous, and known for its snow and rock-slide hazards. Yet whenever the team was in town, we would travel up to our winter home on the Friday night, after work and school, ski on Saturday, and then, snowstorm or not, drive down Saturday for a 5:00 p.m. game in Vancouver, returning to the mountain later that night. Forty years ago, long before cell phones and four-wheel-drive suvs, I recall on more than one occasion being stuck in the dead of night in a snowbank, our vehicle having slid off the icy road in whiteout conditions just short of one of the old wooden bridges. The situation was not so bad when we had won the game.

Over the years, my brother Arthur worked his way up within the hockey operations to become president of Northwest Sports Ltd., the public company that my family of origin controlled, which owned the Vancouver Canucks. Because of my professional credentials, my father asked me to join the board of directors and the audit committee of Northwest Sports Ltd. To those of us at the board level, it became clear that the hockey franchise would need a new home if it was to remain in Vancouver. Management was assigned the task of finding a solution. Once a building site in Vancouver's city center had been identified, designs vetted and bids for construction received, everything was presented to the board. The costs were astronomical. It was obvious that Northwest Sports Ltd. could not afford the debt load that would be required to complete the project, but we recognized something had to happen before our community lost its team.

As I have explained, my parents' legacy commitment to our community and the risk my parents took on behalf of the city's hockey fans were at the core of our family. My brother Arthur approached me and asked if I was willing, in order to not burden the taxpayers, to risk our combined inherited financial resources and pursue the dream of building the city a new home for its beloved Vancouver Canucks, so that future generations could enjoy NHL hockey like we had growing up. Since my values were aligned with those of my parents, my answer was automatic. I said yes.

At the time, unbeknownst to the public, our father's health was failing. Although he was still of sound mind, he no longer had the physical strength to pursue a vision of this magnitude. However, his well-considered succession plan allowed my brother and me to actively strive for our shared dream of stewarding my father's dream: continued ownership of an NHL franchise. To that, my brother and I added our dream of completing the privately financed construction of a twenty-thousand-seat arena and of bringing the NBA to Vancouver. I did not fully realize the significance of what we had achieved until I found myself, as the only female owner, at the side of NBA commissioner David Stern during NBA governors' meetings in New York, being introduced to my fellow NBA club owners. Many of them were members of the Fortune 500. Believe me: I can completely appreciate the power of a dream!

Here is another way of looking at the dreams behind the successful succession of a family business. As business people, we understand that businesses must either grow or shrink. When a healthy business transitions to the next generation, at some point it will plateau. When that happens, it will not be enough for the next generation to simply stick to the status quo, operating the business in the same manner and with the same vision as the prior generation. In today's flattening world, it is only a matter of time before a stagnating family business will come up against the highly energetic dreams of people like John Skinner of Painted Rock Estate Winery, or my father, my brother, and me. Who do you think will win that competition? In other words, any successful family business owner needs the passion, perseverance, and determination of a personally driven dream.

Another question that must be asked about a family business is, "Does the next generation have, or will they have, what is needed to be owners, not just management?" The roles and responsibilities of ownership are much different than those of management. Our business schools are solid places to study the trade of management, but ownership is an art: the art of entrepreneurship. It provides strategic direction while balancing risk and reward. Ownership sets the business's vision. Management's task is to implement it. When it comes to a transitioned family business, ownership is even more challenging, since the next generation is stewarding the dreams of a past generation while reinvigorating the business with their own entrepreneurial spirit and dreams.

In one example of failed family ownership, a high-profile takeover battle occurred in 2007 between the discreet Bancroft family, owners of Dow Jones & Co., the publisher of *The Wall Street Journal,* and Rupert Murdoch, the acquisitive media tycoon. For over a hundred years, Dow Jones had remained a family company. However, as the business passed to later generations, the aptitude for ownership disappeared, replaced by an aptitude for dividends. As owners, the Bancroft family shareholders should have been providing strategic direction for the company. Instead, there were times under later generations when the dividend demands and payments from the company surpassed their profits.

In an e-mail sent in the days before the sale, and then also published in *The Wall Street Journal,* one family member, Crawford Hill, explained to his family what he saw as the primary causes of their ownership failure: "Our real legacy was an inherited lack of awareness as to what it takes to nurture, and pass on an effective legacy about, what is really required to be responsible, engaged and active owners of a family business." He continued, "Such things can never be taken for granted—they must be actively nurtured, cultivated, questioned, tested and honed. That has not happened in our family in any meaningful way... There has absolutely never existed any kind of family-wide/cross-branch culture of teaching what it means to be an active, engaged owner, and more crucially, a family director."

Without the passionate dreams of an active and engaged ownership to guide it, a company is like a ship lost at sea, with no clear destination. Management too is left adrift. A family business in such a state is only one competitive economic storm away from ruination.

Perhaps, in your family's analysis, the family business does not fit with its future vision of itself, or the answers to both of the questions above are no and a decision is made to sell the family business. Even if the facts are clear and the decision obvious, selling the family business can still be a stressful decision to make. Seldom is it as straightforward as analyzing the financials, fielding the right offer, and hitting the bid. I would have found it useful to be prepared for the emotional nature of this decision in my family. Many facets of my experience are common among other families when the family business has come to represent the core of the family. This means that for some family members, the business has defined who they are, cemented business relationships, and connected them to the community as well as to one another.

Having also inherited my father's love of numbers, I was aware of the personal financial risk I had assumed by investing in a sports and entertainment organization. Entering into this partnership was what some might have called a financial kamikaze mission, and I kept a watchful eye on the financial projections. Before long, economic indicators such as rising interest rates and the falling Canadian dollar, along with an NHL lockout on the horizon—the first of many to come—were signaling the need for substantial future cash injections from us as owners to sustain operations. I knew there was only one correct business decision to make. The game was going to be too expensive for me. It was becoming a game for billionaires. But how could I sell without feeling like I was betraying my family and my community?

After everything my brother and I had been through together, from the highs of beginning construction to the lowest point, the death of our father, I had to have the "other talk" with him. I had to deliver the message that this dream of ours had run aground. We had to wake up, smell the coffee, and sell our interest. It was time for someone else to steward the community franchise. It was an emotionally charged conversation. I remember it as if it happened yesterday. Arthur and I met privately at GM Place. We walked into the darkened arena in the middle of the day and sat in the empty stands. As the face and the driving force of the organization, my brother had done it.

He had quieted the naysayers, those who are quick to tear down the dreams of others. Yet here I was, his younger sister, confirming what I suspect he already knew.

With understandable emotion, he said, "I can't sell. My dream is that one day my children will work alongside me here, as I did with our father." Since that was the case, I sold my interest to our trusted partner John McCaw. I will be forever grateful to have had, outside of my family, two men of unequivocal integrity in Mr. McCaw and his advisor Stan McCammon. Arthur eventually followed me in selling to Mr. McCaw. He could have hung on until the end, but no one does themselves or their family any favors by loving their business to death.

Including the younger Family Bank members in ongoing family discussions will ensure that any future expectations of working in the family business are realistic. It is not uncommon, for example, for young family members to select a particular educational path as a foundation for a future role of some sort in the family business. Unless a family discusses such matters openly, these younger family members may feel the rug has been pulled out from under them if a decision is made to sell the family business. A family using the Family Bank approach recognizes that the relationships of family members with one another and with the world around them are closely intertwined with the family business. Engaging in conversations about the financial future of that business will help prepare the next generation to make the correct decisions, however emotionally difficult they may be, and ready them for a future that potentially does not include the current family business.

IN FURTHER assessing your family's financial assets, you need to be realistic, sensible, and pragmatic, and getting a grip on one's financial assets should be a straightforward activity. However, some of the experts who advise people on financial matters have needlessly confused the assessment process. With the growing ability of computers to process large amounts of information, particularly numbers, and to perform complex calculations and projections, a new breed of advisor has been created. But their complex financial projections should come with an easy-to-understand warning message. Projections are simply forecasts, and as with a weather forecast, the longer the range of view, the less reliable the forecast. This crucial information should appear as a message to clients at the beginning, in the middle, and at the end of every financial projection. Instead, it is relegated to pages of fine print at the end of the report that most clients do not read.

These financial forecasts are based on assumptions—*tons* of assumptions. For instance, some programs will take a family's current financial position and project it out over ten, twenty, thirty or more years, based on input provided by the client. Well, have you ever heard the expression "garbage in, garbage out"? If the financial program is fed incorrect information, the imbedded calculations will be incorrect, as will the resulting projection. No one really knows what the future holds. If a client provides the information on what they believe they will be spending on an annual basis in the future to support their future lifestyle and the financial planner asks the textbook questions to clarify the numbers, the final input could be rubbish.

In addition, the sophisticated computer programs used by financial planners are based on static algorithms, which means the underlying factors in the calculations are largely fixed. This is the case, for instance, when it comes to the program's calculation of the taxes to be paid in each projected year of the plan. The tax impact is calculated based on current tax rates, yet it is unreasonable to assume that tax rates are never going to change in the future.

These complex financial projections can also mess with a family's psychology regarding money and perceived financial wealth. At a client's request, I reviewed a twenty-six-page PowerPoint report based on one long-term forecast. I understand the nature of these projections but it was easy to see how any family could have been swept up in the results. This was the scenario. The family had set aside significant retirement funds in investment accounts and owned, mortgage free, a substantial family home. This home, which the financial planner had put into the financial projection, was valued at $1 million. That amount is reasonable in the family's marketplace today, but the financial plan had projected it to be worth $26 million thirty years in the future. Based on this projection, the family was advised to establish trusts for their children. Oh, and by the way, the report stated, the trust department of the company the financial planner worked for could do that for them. The report also recommended the family purchase insured investments through the company's investment department, establish two wills, establish a private foundation, meet with the private banking department, etc. Seriously, there were twenty-six pages of this stuff correlated to a $26 million future projected value of their home. For a million dollars a page, perhaps you too could get a computer to give you this advice. A more cynical person looking at this report might suggest that the advisor was being incentivized to cross-sell for every other department of their company.

Financial projections can be useful, as long as they are taken with a giant grain of salt. They can show what happens to one's financial position when key underlying factors change, such as the rate of return or the inflation rate, and when adjustments are made, through sudden injections or withdrawals of large sums of money. Rather than using these projections as a reason to buy protection products, however, families who are successfully transitioning multigenerational financial wealth will use them as what my statistical analysis university professor would call "sensitivity analysis tools."

Otherwise, you are at the mercy of the number manipulators and the emotive language they use to sell you their products. Often saying they are helping you to protect your legacy, or to prevent loss of financial assets or even a broken family, they promote the sale of the very products that are so often found in failed succession and wealth-transition plans.

Families who utilize the Family Bank approach will not fall victim to advisors who prey on their fear or ego to sell them unnecessary trusts, private foundation structures, insurance, or guaranteed investment products. Instead, through the Family Bank process, they will develop a clear idea of who they are today and how they want to see themselves in the future. Whether or not there is a belief or knowledge that there will be significant financial assets to transition, the family following the Family Bank approach will, through ongoing communication built on trust within the family, be preparing the next generation, no matter their financial journey, for their future roles and responsibilities, and clearly managing their expectations vis-à-vis the Family Bank through the family's shared vision.

# 7

# A COMMON HOT BUTTON:
## The Family Cottage

IT IS ONE OF those perfect days at the cottage, an idyllic summer retreat resonant with family memories. As you relax with a cool drink and a good book in the setting sun, you fondly remember the days when your young children eagerly anticipated roasting marshmallows around an open fire, fun-filled game nights and laughter over shared family dinners. The memories are powerful and emotional. Now, things seem more poignant than ever before. You think about your now grown children and perhaps your grandchildren, fearing they may one day face the loss of the cottage that has played such a significant role in weaving the fabric of your family. Is this asset going to serve second- and third-generation Family Bank members as it did you?

Here is where I insert a warning: be careful with this sentimentality. It is exactly this kind of evocative picture many professionals paint in an attempt to sell you their products. They take cunning advantage of the strong human emotions surrounding family. Every summer, these professionals produce an onslaught of glossy information circulars that promote trusts, corporations, and insurance policies all ostensibly aimed at averting the tragic loss of the beloved family cottage. Families using the Family Bank approach, however, are armed with the knowledge that the family cottage will be assessed like the family's other financial assets. Its genuine value will be measured against the shared vision your family has developed.

Estate-planning advisors, whether dealing with accounting, legal, or financial aspects, commonly recommend trusts as a way to protect against the loss of the family cottage. These advisors are referring to the actual loss of the family cottage if the family members must sell it in order to pay estate taxes upon the death of the owner. In Canada, a tax becomes payable on the property when the property owner dies, based on a capital gain. This gain is calculated as the difference between the original cost of the property, plus any enhancements, and the fair market value of the property at the time of the owner's death. Using a common scenario, a family cottage owned by the parents over a period of fifty years or so, and enjoyed by their children, their children's spouses, and their grandchildren during that time, can generate a significant tax bill for the parents' estate. This situation has created some financial concern for families, since the cost of recreational properties in many regions has increased substantially over the last fifty years.

The general theory behind using a trust structure is that by putting the family cottage in a trust, the tax can be deferred. Note I said deferred here, though, not eliminated. Deferring the tax on the cottage does not mean the tax is permanently avoided. Under current Canadian tax laws, it means that the tax will be due in twenty-one years, at the tax rates applicable then. So, while you may be protecting an asset of the Family Bank for a few years, by placing your cottage in a trust, you are also creating a future liability.

All of this complex tax-driven work can easily end up being a waste of time, effort, and money. It has been said that only two things in life are certain: death and taxes. I would add a third certainty to that list: tax laws will change. Here is a personal example. My parents built our family ski cabin when I was very young. My father was a clever CA and an enormous proponent of tax-planning structures in their early, less complicated days. As a result, our family cabin was rolled into a corporation on a tax-advantaged basis, with my siblings and me as the sole equal common shareholders. It certainly made practical sense at the time. But guess what happened? The tax laws changed. We learned the hard way that tax laws are not written in stone. The Canada Revenue Agency (CRA) created a new ruling on items they termed personal-use properties (PUPs). Sounds cute and cuddly, right? Just what every young woman wants? Wrong. Not this young woman, because as a full-time, non-income-producing university student, the CRA required me to pay sizeable taxes on a property that I seldom benefited from. I was too busy pursuing my dream of becoming a CA.

Because of subsequent changes in the tax laws, a corporation is no longer considered to be an appropriate structure for a PUP like the family cottage. Nonetheless, the trust structure is still widely supported. To some, the idea sounds secure and infallible: "setting up a family trust to protect the family cottage for future generations." Families following the Family Bank approach, however, will consider the problems that can arise when a trust's beneficiaries are bound together for the duration of the trust under the direction of the trustees. They will be prepared for the roles and responsibilities, beyond those of an administrative nature, of both trustees and beneficiaries in using a complicated trust structure successfully.

Additionally, families who adopt the Family Bank model understand the importance of clear and frank communication. They have had some practice negotiating and working together to set a vision for the family, solving problems along the way. That means they are better prepared to consider the vast array of questions that can cause discord when discussing how siblings might share the family cottage. How will the summer weekends be divided? What is the guest policy? What is the pet policy? Will the costs of maintaining the cottage be divided equally (per sibling or per total in each sibling family unit) or be based on usage? How will cottage staples like toilet paper and laundry soap be managed? Who will finance breakages, repairs, and maintenance? Family Bank members working continually to strengthen communication and trust within the family will be equipped to answer these potentially thorny questions as they come up.

For some families, questions that seem simple often become the most serious sticking points once second-generation family members try to find a way to work together. For instance, maybe one sibling always takes the bookings calendar for the ski cabin and fills in every weekend, to the exclusion of everyone else. If the siblings are able to move past that sort of selfish behavior, they will come to the realization that fair and equal are not synonymous. For instance, one sibling always taking Christmas week at the ski cabin may not be fair to other siblings if they all live in a city nearby, but may be fair if it is the only time that sibling, who lives in another country, can travel to the destination.

Family Bank members will already have a firm understanding of this fact. As a family, they will have agreed to relevant policies to address such issues long before they are needed. In contrast, imagine the desolate scenario in which siblings who have fought over the family cottage for years come together following the death of their parents only to break up the family cottage trust and sell the property.

Another way that advisors use scare tactics in regards to what happens to the family cottage is by suggesting you buy insurance to protect this asset in the future. Insurance agents often use language like "your primary concern" to refer to the potential capital gains tax due when your cottage is sold or inherited. They point out that another way outside of deferring this tax payment is to set up a spousal rollover on your death. However, they continue, at the time of your spouse's death, this tax bill will need to be paid and the taxes owing will be calculated on the deemed value of the property at that time.

The trap is set! Your family is then asked how they plan on paying this eventual tax bill. The agents crunch numbers based on current tax laws and estimated future valuations to convince you that insurance is the answer. I beg to differ. My husband and I had conversations with insurance agents regarding our family cottage years ago, when our sons were still quite young. Even with our emotional attachment to the property factored in, I was unable to fathom the idea of making a significant annual cash payment to an insurance agent and company based on an insurance policy that would mature at a very distant date. Nothing is certain, I mused to myself—the policy was based on a significant number of uncertain variables used to create a long-range forecast. While the forecast was useful, I knew we needed to take it with a grain of salt. Insurance companies are in the business of making money, and the only certain winners in this scenario were the insurance agent and the insurance company.

Many years later, as we took an evening walk, my then nineteen-year-old son asked me why we owned a vacant property close to our family cottage. This is exactly the kind of question that allows my husband and me, as Family Bank leaders, to prepare our children to become responsible stewards of the family's financial assets.

I described to my son the decision-making process regarding the cottage that his father and I had gone through when he and his brother were young. I used our conversation as an opportunity both to discuss money issues and to strengthen our ties of open, honest communication. While appreciating there is not necessarily a right or a wrong answer, I walked him through the process of our Family Bank's decision making.

In stewarding our family's assets, I explained, my husband and I are always re-examining our overall investment strategy as it relates to our family's shared future. This includes an alignment of our financial capital objectives with our risk appetite. Consequently, our Family Bank's investments are not limited to the financial markets. In the spirit of prudence and successful multigenerational planning, we also invest in real estate property, other businesses, and collectibles. Accordingly, when we considered the acquisition of the vacant lot close to our family cottage, it first had to meet our Family Bank's requirements for raw land investing. I explained to my son why this property was a fit.

In addition to fitting within our Family Bank's investment parameters for raw land, this property had other potential benefits. One day, the acquisition might make it possible for us to leave a property to each son, rather than leaving them a shared property. Perhaps, if our family was approached to sell our cottage at a price we simply could not refuse, we could build another family cottage on this additional property. Perhaps this additional property could be considered a hedge against future property tax, since it could be sold and the proceeds used to pay the tax due on a deemed disposition of the family cottage upon the death of the last owner. From a business perspective, I told my son, it made more sense for our Family Bank to purchase an appreciating asset with the Family Bank's financial capital rather than invest the sunk cash outlays in an elusive insurance policy. Over the long term, the property would continue to provide our Family Bank with more investment opportunities and financial flexibility.

The information I imparted to my son and later shared with his brother required considerable thought and digestion on their parts. Such knowledge allows them to build the financial acuity they will require as they enter adulthood and prepare for their future roles and responsibilities as stewards of our Family Bank.

I intentionally left the two most important points for last, though. These were not new messages in our Family Bank conversations. They were ideas we often now discuss at the family dinner table, especially with regard to our cherished family cottage.

The first point is that careful planning is imperative. Our sons need to agree on policies related to operating, maintaining, and financing the cottage long before these policies are actually needed. That includes future marital considerations. Otherwise, this asset that was once happily shared by our family could end up being the asset that divides our sons as brothers and family.

The other point is that, as the future owners and stewards of the Family Bank, our sons may decide there is a more prudent way to deploy this financial asset. At some stage, it might make sense to sell this property and invest the funds elsewhere. My husband and I emphasized that this was completely acceptable to us. It is never wise to endow the family cottage with a meaning to which it is not entitled, nor to allow any building or property to become a financial burden or a strain on relationships within the family. The vital message here is that the true value of the family cottage is not in the mortar and bricks of it as a financial asset, but in the time we have spent there together creating shared family memories. We created those memories as individual family members; the cottage itself did not create them.

By clearly articulating our shared values and our vision of ourselves as a family, my family can be confident we will not wander unknowingly into the emotional traps laid by estate-planning product sellers. With or without this cottage, we will continue to share the family memories that have created our sense of belonging and pride in the family. As the sun dips below the horizon, we are content to know that, whatever the future holds, our Family Bank members will continue to generate shared memories wherever and whenever we jointly agree to gather and enjoy special family time.

# 8

## TRUSTS:

## Not Necessarily the Be-All and End-All of Succession and Wealth-Transition Plans

BASED ON my personal experience as a dynastic beneficiary, a trustee, and a professional CA and Investment Advisor, I can affirm that a trust is a brilliant tool when used in the manner for which it was originally intended. Some family members will not have the personal characteristics required to become stewards of the Family Bank. In this instance, trusts can be used effectively to protect the Family Bank's beneficiaries from outside parties or from themselves.

One classic example is the wealthy elderly widow who is unable to say no to relentless requests for cash from ne'er-do-well children. In such a case, a trust structure is very useful. Without the protection of a trust entity that allows trustees to say no on her behalf, this woman's fortune could be drained away by her "Gucci loafer" and "Prada pump" children, leaving her struggling to make ends meet while they enjoy the good life.

Another scenario involves the use of a trust to protect its beneficiaries from themselves, including those who are incapable of managing their own affairs. In my work, I have seen this apply also to the elderly "child" who has demonstrated over a lifetime an inability to manage financial wealth. Simply put, the family member hemorrhages cash. Even if a Family Bank is established, the opportunity to prepare a mature adult like this to become a steward of the Family Bank has long since passed.

It is interesting to me that, in all my research on this subject matter, James E. Hughes Jr. is the only writer I have come across who thoroughly explains how we use these structures incorrectly. But despite the information being readily available, accountants and lawyers continue to provide copious amounts of information highlighting the selling points—from their perspective. In addition to tax minimization and deferment, some of the other reasons routinely given for establishing a trust include avoiding probate fees, simplifying estate administration, increasing confidentiality, and protecting against estate litigation. Yet we now know that succession plans do not fail for any of those reasons. In fact, my experience has shown me that many people do not understand the real brilliance of a trust structure.

Trusts were originally intended to create "a suspended period of ownership." The financial assets that the grantor puts into a trust are to be managed by trustees and owned by the trust until the beneficiaries are prepared for ownership. Trusts were never intended as a way to control beneficiaries or to minimize taxes.

History shows us why trusts originated. For instance, during the twelfth and thirteenth centuries, many male landowners in European countries left to fight in the Crusades. Their wives were not permitted to own property at the time, so ownership of the family's lands was suspended by allocating them into a trust structure. This trust was managed by another man, for the benefit of the family, until the crusader's return from battle. Fortunately, the world has evolved substantially over the last several centuries. Women are permitted to directly own assets, thereby eliminating the need of a trust when men pursue activities that put their lives at risk.

While ownership based on gender is no longer an issue, a trust does have an important role for multigenerational transitions when it comes to what should be occurring during this suspended period of ownership. This is the interval during which the trustees' critical role is to mentor the beneficiaries. An excellent example of this occurred during the reign of Louis XV of France in the 1700s. When the Sun King, Louis XIV, died, his heir to the throne was only five years old. Fortunately, Louis XIV had drafted a new will the year prior to his death. This will appointed a group of trustees, a council of sage individuals, to govern France until Louis XV came of age. The lead trustee and president of the council was Philippe II, Duke of Orléans, who was magnificent in his role. With the utmost care and attention, he mentored and prepared young Louis XV for his roles and responsibilities as the future king of France. Upon reaching maturity, Louis XV, who became known as Louis the Well Beloved, ruled for almost sixty years, until his death in 1774. During that time, France maintained its position as a world power.

A truly effective trust establishes a relationship in which trustees see their most important role as mentoring, and beneficiaries see theirs as learning. Of course, trustees must competently administer the trust, but they must remain clear that the structure exists as a way of suspending ownership of assets until the beneficiaries are sufficiently prepared to take them over.

However, in my experience, lawyers most often suggest trusts to their clients for control purposes. One argument commonly made is that a trust is the best way to postpone wealth transference to the next generation until younger family members are "better prepared" for the financial realities of the twenty-first century. (Now that was an easy sale!)

Stop! Think! That won't happen unless something concrete is done to help prepare these young family members for wealth transference. The snag arises with the appointment of the trustees. Trustees today are seldom appointed as trusted mentors to the beneficiary. In fact, this aspect of the trustee's role is often not even addressed. Today's trustees are typically selected on the basis of being competent administrators, prudent investors, and reliable check writers, with little or no thought being given to the mentorship role.

In a common scenario, a corporate big bank trustee is appointed as the sole trustee. This was my experience. Around my thirtieth birthday, I was sent to the big bank trust company to receive a lump-sum payment from my maternal grandparents' dynastic trust. Both the existence of the trust and the lump-sum payment came as a complete surprise to me. I was more fortunate than many inheritors in that I had pursued a professional career as a CA. My education, in combination with my marriage to a fellow CA who had long before transitioned his career to the investment industry, provided me with the financial acuity to manage my inheritance. Otherwise, I could easily have become a statistic—one of the 70 percent who lose control of their inheritance.

Another argument made by the legal profession in support of trusts is that a trust can be used as a vehicle to provide an ongoing income stream to the beneficiaries. Sounds good, doesn't it? However, there is a wrinkle in this approach that is not commonly discussed. Using a trust in this way can create what some refer to as a "trust fund baby": a person who spends their life waiting around for their trust fund checks. An unintended consequence of using a trust to provide an income stream is that beneficiaries can become remittance-addicted, and victims of a state of mind known as entitlement.

There was a time in history when trusts were designed to live on forever. The income stream generated from these perpetual trusts created a permanent leisure class. Out of love, grantors wanted to help the next generation by providing an easier life for them. They wanted their children to be happy. The irony is that perfectly capable people who become dependent on financial handouts can easily slip into a role where they do not pursue independent work or a purposeful life. And a life of entitlement, one they do not financially control for themselves and is without purpose, is not a happy one!

As a part of my ongoing professional development, I attend an assortment of professional seminars every year. Recently, I attended one led by a tax lawyer who specialized in trusts. The room was full of accountants, and the seven-hour seminar was predominantly focused on the current tax issues around trust structures in our jurisdiction. However, the seminar outline indicated there would also be a section on why and when trusts should be used. When he got to that section, at around 2:00 p.m. on a Friday afternoon, the instructor spent less than twenty minutes on the topic. Basically, he advised us that trusts are predominantly used for wealth transitions and that a family is "negligent" if it does not use one. Before moving on, the instructor asked if there were any questions. I politely spoke up. "How successful are these structures in preventing an involuntary loss of the assets through things like inattention, incompetence, mismanagement, foolish expenditures, and family feuding?" I asked. Poor fellow, he was stunned. He had no clue what I was talking about. Somewhere along the way, this tax lawyer had missed the message about the continued failure rate of succession and wealth-transition plans that are dominated by trusts.

The Family Bank approach turns this control model upside down. Rather than trying to control the next generation, it focuses specifically on preparing the next generation to competently control their own lives. The Family Bank approach supports the development of hard-working, productive, responsible individuals who have earned the right to feel capable and are secure in the knowledge they can make good decisions. As a result, Family Bank leaders can spend their golden years being proud of these younger members rather than worrying about controlling them now and from beyond the grave.

The accounting profession takes another tack on trusts. As a businessperson, a financial advisor, and a taxpayer, I certainly appreciate the value of potential tax savings. Furthermore, our tax code is increasing in complexity, and many professional accountants have built highly respected careers specializing in taxation. However, I want to sound a few notes of caution—points that are seldom raised when it comes to succession planning.

The first point is that the tax planning you pay a lot for today, in relation to a succession or wealth-transition plan, will likely become useless as a result of future changes to our tax laws. Given the ever-increasing spending by governments, we will likely not see an easing off in the taxes we pay. On the contrary, what we pay in taxes will increase—and the changes will start with the government closing all the loopholes our clever tax professionals squeeze us through. And while there is never a good time to deal with the hassles created by changes in tax laws, it is definitely not a desired retirement activity.

Imagine relocating in your retirement years to a sunny location while the winters are cold back home. One day, you receive a phone call from the person who has been handling your mail. A letter from the tax authorities has arrived. Suddenly, the sun feels a little prickly. Knowing that you will not be back in the snow for a few weeks yet, you ask the person on the other end of the line to open the letter and read you what it says.

The document is a notice of reassessment and audit covering the years during which your accountants used some creative tax planning, maybe involving trust structures, for succession and wealth-transition purposes. If you wish to appeal the reassessment, the letter says you have two weeks to respond to the notice. You spend the next couple of days trying to reach the taxman to explain that you are out of the country and will not be back for a few more weeks. They grant you an extension. Whew! You dodged that solar flare-up. Yet for the remainder of your stay in the sunny clime, you are haunted by the thought of a tax audit awaiting you back home. When you return, you diligently pull all your files and receipts together and send them off to the tax department. "Done," you think. Ah, but not quite. The fun is just beginning.

No news is good news, right? Because you have not heard anything further from the tax department, you think you have cleared the audit. However, while they put the time pressure on you, there is no sense of urgency on their side. Out of the blue, you receive another letter. The auditors want to meet with you. They have questions. It feels a bit like a game of cat and mouse but you have no choice. In the end, these bureaucrats may or may not find they have reason to reassess you based on their audit. In the meantime, it feels like you are in a very tight corner.

The big banks are the newer players in the trust service industry. In Canada, the big banks have bought out many traditional trust companies, and along with their increased capacity to conveniently sell us products comes the apparent loss of trustees serving as mentors. Judging by the sheer force of the big banks' advertising campaigns and their built-in internal pressures to sell their trust services, independent trust companies seem to have almost disappeared. But some still do exist. Sometimes it just takes a little hunting to find them.

I was recently asked by a client to make a recommendation on the appointment of a family trustee. Unfortunately, there were no family members either able or willing to take on the task themselves. Safeguarding the privacy of my client, I interviewed all of the corporate trustees I could find in our city, including those at the big banks. This is what I discovered. One big bank would not even meet with me after I indicated that there was the potential for a trust battle in the family in the future. They made it clear that they would not deal with anything messy. Another big bank would only consider the account if the trust account was what they called "big enough." Another big bank said it would consider the account, but only if the assets in the family's investment portfolio, which was managed by their family's trusted portfolio manager elsewhere, was transferred to this big bank instead. It became clear that for all the big banks, trust services were based on the easy fees generated by fuss-free trusts, with the assets deposited in the bank's own accounts.

The good news is that I eventually found a traditional corporate trustee whose business model was intentionally independent of any bank. This kind of professional trustee tends to the specific needs of the family, undertaking both quantitative and qualitative tasks as needed. While traditional trustees can offer independent referrals to other professionals, they encourage families to maintain the trusted relationships they have established with their own lawyers, accountants, and financial advisors.

As an investment professional myself, I wholeheartedly agree that big bank trust companies must be prudent when making their investment decisions. That may not serve their clients' best interests, however. In relation to my inherited trust portfolio, the bank took what amounted to no risk, never straying far from guaranteed investment certificates (GICs) and term deposits. As a result, in comparison to the world's financial markets at the time, and taking into account the easy guaranteed fees the bank collected from my account and inflation, the portfolio declined.

Dynamic wealth creators often take great risks in bringing their dreams to life. A big bank trustee will invest in the opposite way, and the result may be, as in my case, a gradual erosion of the capital. This is not to say that financial wealth being transitioned through a trust structure should be invested in a high-risk manner. However, it is advisable to find a trusted investment advisor with deep expertise and experience in long-term wealth preservation. Such an investment advisor understands and is able to implement the mandate to both safeguard and prudently grow your investments.

Finally, families relying on a trust for their succession and wealth-transition planning may miss something crucial. As we have learned, for 60 percent of the succession plans that fail it is due to a breakdown in communication and trust within the family. Many trusts today are akin to an arranged marriage, in which the grantor selects the trustees (most likely lawyers, accountants, and the big bank trust companies), identifies the beneficiaries, and, without cross-consultation, commits the two groups to a trust relationship. Like operagoers and punk rockers, however, these two groups of individuals are often on very different journeys in life, and may be unable or unwilling to communicate with one another.

As noted earlier, 25 percent of succession plans also break down due to "unprepared heirs"—in this scenario, beneficiaries who are unprepared for the financial realities of the twenty-first century. It is well worth repeating that if trustees are not conscientiously preparing beneficiaries to assume ownership of the assets, and the beneficiaries do not recognize that as the responsibility of the trustees, the beneficiaries will remain unprepared for eventual ownership.

Finally, 12 percent of succession and wealth-transition plans fail because the family lacks a shared vision. If the family does not agree to the purpose of the trust, this can result in visits to litigators by beneficiaries who want to sue the trustees, which I've seen on more than one occasion, in order to break up the trust.

Remember: the loss of your financial capital due to foolish expenditures does not refer only to gambled-away weekends in Las Vegas. Foolish expenditures can also include the cost of the initial set-up of a trust and the ongoing fees paid to lawyers, accountants, and big bank trust companies for the required meetings, financial statement preparation, filing of tax returns, operation, and maintenance a trust requires. When trusts are utilized without addressing the qualitative reasons why succession plans fail, the only financial winners will be all those professionals.

If everyone understands from the outset the intended purpose of a trust in your Family Bank, and if all Family Bank members agree to the selection of respected trustees and appreciate the important role of trustees as mentors to the beneficiaries, your trust may well meet your Family Bank's goals, whatever they may be. In the final analysis, however, a label that reads as follows should be attached to trust structures:

WARNING: Proceed With Caution.
Think twice before using complex structures like trusts.

# 9

# PHILANTHROPY:
## A Family Bank Affair

I T IS A GLAMOROUS evening. The who's who of the city have gathered, the men in black tie and the women in elegant evening gowns, showing off jewels that would rival those of any royal family. My parents, other family members, and I are attending a gala in recognition of my father's philanthropic activities. We are seated at one of the head tables and I am enraptured by the words of tribute and the video presentation showcasing my father's accomplishments. In my late teens, I adore my father. Now, for the first time, I am catching a glimpse of him through the eyes of our community. There is a sense of awe in the room with regard to his remarkable humanitarianism. I am only a young girl, but already I feel a growing sense of moral obligation to follow in the footsteps of this extraordinary role model.

Thirty years ago, philanthropic conversations seldom occurred at family dinner tables, and infrequently at ours. In fact, I barely remember my father being at the dinner table during the week, due to his ethic of hard work and his long hours at the office. However, if we had known then about the Family Bank approach, our weekend time together would no doubt have included regular discussions on the subject.

Many families utilizing the Family Bank approach include genuine caring and concern for others in their shared vision. As a result, philanthropy is part of fulfilling that vision. Following the Family Bank approach, the deployment of family financial assets for philanthropic purposes requires a joint decision by all the family members, whatever their ages. This joint family activity provides a forum for the family members to practise their teamwork as they work together with the shared goal of giving back to their community or the world at large. And it can be a lightning rod of positive change in strengthening communication within the family. Further, making philanthropic decisions together will help prepare the next generation for their future roles as stewards of the Family Bank's assets.

Philanthropy is usually among the least contentious issues for a family to discuss. As a result, these conversations provide a supportive venue in which to teach the youngest members of the family about family values, like caring for others, stewardship, and teamwork. Taking a more formal approach to philanthropic activities also allows older Family Bank members to assess whether the family is willing and able to work as a team.

Furthermore, a shared philanthropic undertaking can also have a way of reconnecting families. For families who have sold the business that once defined them, philanthropy can be the means by which they reestablish themselves and gain a new identity in the community.

The first lesson I learned from the early death of my father was not to delay having important family conversations. My husband and I began philanthropic discussions with our sons when they were very young, encouraging them to collect change in their Unicef boxes at Halloween and to take food to school for donation to the local food bank. As my sons matured, the nature of our shared philanthropic activities became more formalized, along with our expectations for those activities.

My sons now understand that, like any business investment, a philanthropic investment requires a purposeful plan.
That plan begins with defining our philanthropic objectives.
As my husband and I have pointed out during family discussions, many not-for-profit organizations hire fundraisers who
are exceptional at their jobs. Some of them have actually even
earned certificates in the field of fundraising. However, rather
than being sold someone else's philanthropic objectives, every
family needs to identify its own.

Naturally, we do not let dinner conversations on the subject
end that easily. We are fortunate that our 6-foot-8 and 6-foot-4
sons still enjoy home-cooked meals, and are willing to participate in these discussions, as long as there is still food on
the table. Over the years, my husband and I have passed along
everything we know about the who, what, when, where, and
why of philanthropic decisions.

The why was the simplest question to answer. We clarified
what it means for a family to be obligated with respect to philanthropy. To paraphrase the famous biblical passage, from
those to whom much is given, much is required. My sons know
now that what our family has been given is not defined solely
by our financial capital; it also includes our human and intellectual capital. We give to the larger community not only by
donating money but also by donating our unique skills and
our time. For examples to follow, our sons had to look no far-
ther than their father and me. Both of us have donated our
financial and investment expertise to a variety of not-for-profit
organizations.

When it comes to donating money, we explained to our sons
that there are essential differences between giving, charity,
and philanthropy. Giving is what you do when someone knocks
on your door asking for a donation. Not a lot of thought or planning goes into that giving. Charity is the capital you donate

because you are genuinely interested in easing the suffering of others. Philanthropy, on the other hand, requires research, thoughtful consideration, and analysis. A philanthropic decision is akin to a business decision, except that the philanthropist's return on investment is measured by the good the capital does for the chosen charitable organization, rather than by an increase in the earnings per share. In our Family Bank, all four members decide the specific dollar amount, and we place great value on thoughtful consideration in support of the donation.

As they got the hang of the ongoing conversation, our sons wondered as to "when" they should begin. We quickly pointed out that they have been involved with helping others, in some respect, for most of their lives. Going back to their preschool years, they have regularly shown genuine caring and concern for others, and acted upon it. We made it clear that every donation—whether of human, intellectual, or financial capital—is needed, appreciated, and makes a difference.

The "who" question was where it got interesting. Over time, we agreed that any joint philanthropic activities had to take us in a direction the majority of us agreed upon. As an example, I explained to my sons that my mother and father, their grandparents, had determined that children would be their area of focus, recognizing the critical importance of supporting and developing youth. This was in the days when orphanages still existed, so they began donating to a community orphans' fund. This choice resonated with my parents at the time. As I explained to my sons, their role as Family Bank members is to get involved with something that resonates personally for them in the twenty-first century.

We discussed the "where" issue over several conversations, in conjunction with the "who." The first element of "where" was relatively easy. We asked our sons, "Do you want to focus your philanthropic efforts locally, regionally, nationally, and/or globally?" And then we added, "Do you want to support a spe-cific person, a cause, an event, or an umbrella organization?" These were excellent questions for them to consider.

The second element my husband and I suggested my sons reflect on was the nature of the organization. Would they con-sider a fledgling not-for-profit or only mature, widely recog-nized organizations? Through our discussions, they learned that, just like a financial investment in a start-up company, an investment in a young not-for-profit organization was a higher risk. The new charity might be here this year and gone next year. At the same time, investment in a higher-risk organiza-tion might be more rewarding, since each donation could make a significant difference to the organization's survival, and hence to those in need. On the flip side, well-established blue-chip charities are generally more stable in their operations, and therefore can be considered a lower risk. Your donation may not make as large an impact on the direct recipients of such a char-ity, however, since there is a greater likelihood of your donation funding overhead costs. My sons learned that there are no right or wrong answers here, just some issues that responsible phi-lanthropists need to consider.

Because my husband and I are both CAs, we have also engaged our sons in discussions about the financial statements of the charitable organizations in which they have expressed interest. We always encourage them to consider the finan-cial health of the operations when they evaluate the potential riskiness of a not-for-profit organization. Would their finan-cial donation be such a significant portion of the organization's revenues that the organization would be dependent on it? We also encourage them to consider the organization's fundraising methodology to ensure that the organization seeks to be inde-pendent of any particular donor.

Keeping the food coming, and my sons engaged, my hus-band and I have cautioned them about agencies that aim to address a desperate need in the community but may not be able to follow up financially or organizationally. In cases like this, we urge them to seek out a better-managed not-for-profit organization that also addresses that particular need in the community.

As a result of these conversations, my husband, our two sons, and I have developed a specific philanthropic plan for our Family Bank. We have agreed that we will come together as a group at least once a year solely to discuss the family's philanthropy. Now that our boys are older, the process has become more sophisticated.

Our approach is as follows. Each person is assigned a sum of money to donate from the financial assets of our Family Bank. Each of us must, prior to making a donation, bring information about the proposed charity before the other three family members for majority approval, and answer any questions the group poses. When I am feeling feisty, my questions can be more probing. I have even been known to ask if the charity under consideration has a pension plan, and, if so, whether it is a defined benefit or a defined contribution pension plan and who it covers. Doesn't every mother ask these kind of questions? How else are they going to learn about these things? At our philanthropy meeting a year later, the prior year's donations are assessed, with each family member required to present their thoughts on the effects of their own donations.

As a consequence of this process, our sons have gained expertise in vetting philanthropic ventures. With regard to one organization, our younger son reported to the Family Bank that he felt as though he "was on a carousel of misinformation, going around and around in circles" when all he was trying to determine was what percentage of his donation would actually reach those in need. As our sons have matured, their expected input into the process has increased exponentially, along with the allocated size of their donations. This has given them the opportunity to hone their presentation skills in a nurturing environment, rather than waiting until they are in a situation where their job or professional reputation may be on the line. Through the Family Bank process, they acquire the skills to make the best decision possible.

At one point, the four of us considered establishing a formal family foundation. I consulted a lawyer who specialized in this area, and she outlined what would be required to set up and maintain such a structure. The ongoing work included annual legal and accounting filings, a specific charitable mandate the foundation would be locked into, and other various requirements.

Upon review, our Family Bank decided against the foundation. We prefer the flexibility to make changes to our charitable funding as necessary, in a manner that best suits our family's philanthropic plan. Furthermore, we wanted our financial resources to go to the designated recipients, rather than be spent on legal and accounting services. I also voted against the foundation because I knew I would be the one left to do the paper chasing and bookkeeping! By going through this exercise, we came to realize that the most important thing for us, as a team, is to have a shared understanding of our philanthropic goals.

Our family's philanthropic practice has been enlightening for all of us. Our sons take their responsibilities in this area very seriously, giving a great deal of thought to the proposals they bring to the Family Bank. For instance, one of our sons came up with a way to provide assistance to an exceptional young scholar at his university who was struggling to continue his post-secondary education due to financial hardship. Our son established a scholar's award, in a club in which they are both members, recognizing that the student he had identified would be the clear recipient based on his exceptional grade-point average. Through setting up the award, our son allowed this young scholar to earn the financial assistance he needed through his abilities, rather than potentially feel diminished as a "charity case." Furthermore, our son established the award in a manner that guaranteed its continued funding in perpetuity, with or without our family's involvement. Finally, he made it a condition that the award be established anonymously, so there could be no suggestion of him or our family benefiting from the gift.

The consequences of our Family Bank approach to philanthropy have been overwhelmingly positive. Unquestioningly, the primary purpose of philanthropy is to express genuine caring for others. However, the communication and trust within our family are continually strengthened as we work together on our shared philanthropic plan. The process has also proven to be an invaluable teaching and learning mechanism in preparing our sons for successful independent lives and their future responsibilities as Family Bank members. Finally, in gathering annually to discuss our shared philanthropic activities, we have another excuse as a family for enjoying a home-cooked meal together.

# 10

# FAMILY BANK GOVERNANCE

U P TO THIS point, we have established that the foundation of a family's multigenerational succession and wealth transition involves articulating its shared values, creating a shared vision statement, and assessing the assets of the family—human, intellectual, and financial—and explored some structures that can be used. The next question to answer is, "What is the path a family will travel in order to transition the family's capital from today's successful generation to the benefit of future generations?" The answer is that the *path of governance* will be traveled by many generations, beginning with loose and informal arrangements in the first generation, which ultimately evolve to become methodical and formal structures by the third generation.

"Governance" describes how the Family Bank organizes itself to reach a family's shared vision. Interestingly, every family already has some form of governance. Commonly recognized forms of governance in families include an autocracy or dictatorship, where a family is ruled by one family member; an oligarchy, ruled by a few, or perhaps both parents; or a democracy, ruled by many, or perhaps all, of the family members. One of the differences between a family's current form of governance and a Family Bank's is that the latter is created to exist over several generations. Additionally, it's common for a family's governance structure to arise in a haphazard way, often reflecting the way things have been done in prior generations of the family. The governance structure of the Family Bank approach, however, is specifically created, with or without legal structures, to reflect the family's shared vision.

For many reasons, including culture, the age of the family members, and the size of the family, different families are better suited to different forms of governance. In creating your Family Bank's governance structure, you will not necessarily aim for the structure that is deemed the best but rather aim for the governance structure that is best suited to your particular circumstances. For instance, if your Family Bank only has two members, you and your spouse, and you have decided that your financial assets should be transitioned into philanthropic activities, your governance structure might include the establishment of a legal structure, like a private foundation. On the other hand, if your Family Bank is composed of four generations of family members—grandparents, children, grandchildren, and great-grandchildren—your Family Bank governance structure may evolve to include some of the following kinds of structures: a family board, to reinforce the family's values and shared vision; a Family Bank board, to oversee the stewardship, growth, and recirculation of the family's financial assets; a philanthropic board, to coordinate the family's philanthropic endeavors; a junior board, to prepare and educate younger family members about their future roles and responsibilities; and a council of elders, to provide the wisdom and insight that comes from experience.

Again, the specific path of governance a family travels will reflect its unique circumstances. However, I recommend that where possible, and as the family grows in size, it is wise to have some kind of structure but to also remain flexible so that the structures can evolve as the family evolves. Like the family's shared vision statement, the governance structure that will be the most effective will be the one that the family members agree to, not necessarily a legally established governance structure like a legally executed family shareholder agreement.

Of special note, though, every adult should have at least one kind of legally prepared governance structure in their succession or wealth transition plan: a will. Many people think that once they have legally executed a will, and stored it away in a safety deposit box, their estate plan is complete. But a will should not be seen as a static document. As families change, so must their wills. For instance, the will of a single person should be updated upon marriage. The will of a married couple should be updated as children come into the family. The will of a family should change when young children become young adults and then mature adults and then parents themselves, and so on. In the same way, the shape and composition of your Family Bank and its governance structure will change as your family matures and evolves.

As Craig E. Aronoff and John L. Ward explain in their book *Family Business Governance,* "a desire to work together for the general good of the family and the business is the common glue a growing number of family business owners are using to establish a framework for governance—the principles and processes that enable maximization of the potential of both the family and the business." By way of example, Aronoff and Ward note that the Pilgrims headed for New England in the 1600s had a remarkable instinct for self-government, working together for their common good in the New World. This was evidenced by their signing of the Mayflower Compact, which, while lacking legal status, had the strength of common consent and consequently became a benchmark for governing institutions worldwide. Whether or not you utilize legal structures, the Family Bank approach allows members to work together for the common good of the family.

To see how the Family Bank will become formalized over three generations, it would be useful to explore how the path of governance evolves within each generation:

### First Generation: The Owner-Founders

A family's governance structure is usually informal in a family's early years, but it does exist. Typically, with the first generation dedicating a lifetime of work to the financial realization of their dreams, the family falls into a random system of communicating and decision making. Initially, family governance most often takes the shape of an ongoing dialogue over a family meal. This is where the seeds of a common family purpose are sown, and where the family's human, intellectual, and financial assets are discussed, though the family will not always identify them in quite the same way.

If you are a member of your family's first generation, it is important not to get overwhelmed by administrative details concerning governance structures for future generations. You have already done the work that will allow your Family Bank to be created, through building your family's financial assets and encouraging each family member's sense of belonging and pride. It will be the rewarding work of succeeding generations to engage you, the elder generation, in the process of creating formal structures to ensure the successful stewardship of your Family Bank for future generations.

### Second Generation: The Sibling Partnership

The transition to the second generation, represented by what many experts call the sibling partnership, has its own unique set of challenges. One is that it will be the first generation to simultaneously be individual wealth creators with their own dreams and stewards of the Family Bank created by the dreams of the prior generation. In addition to balancing these two roles, the family members face the challenge of having no direct role models for how to operate as siblings in a partnership. While their parents likely worked together as partners, relationships between marital partners, which are chosen, are different from those between siblings, which are not chosen. The approaches to governance requirements at this stage will be critical to laying the foundation for future generations to be able to effectively work together as well.

The importance of good communication built on trust and a shared vision within the family becomes clear at the sibling partnership stage. It is essential that the governance structure facilitates the siblings' ability to learn to work well together as a team. By modeling genuine respect and caring for each other as they tend to the Family Bank's affairs, they significantly improve the chances for a successful transition to the third generation and beyond.

At the sibling partnership level, the governance structure often requires a degree of flexibility. In one family I worked with, first-generation members, the grandparents, had placed a sizeable portion of their liquid assets in a trust for their grandchildren. The trust named the sibling partnership, the parents of these young children, as sharing responsibility equally as trustees for the beneficiaries. The original intent of the first generation members was for significant assets to be turned over to each grandchild as they attained the age of twenty-one. However, as stewards of this wealth, the sibling trustees consulted with one another and agreed that their children would not be prepared as heirs for this level of wealth, and its accompanying responsibility, at such a young age. With the common goal of stewarding the family's assets on behalf of the beneficiaries, the siblings jointly agreed to delay the transition of these assets to an age at which their children would be better prepared to receive such an inheritance.

## Third Generation: The Cousin Consortium

As time passes, families get bigger. As in operating a business, there is usually a tipping point at which the governance structure of a family must evolve from being informal to being a more formal structure. As a rule, a formalized structure is usually required once a family reaches a size of ten to fifteen members. This situation most often occurs when the family is transitioning its financial wealth, in whatever form that takes, to the third generation: the cousin consortium.

I would not be honest if I said this transition to the third generation is a simple process. However, it need not be a difficult one. The problem is that, in our culture, we do not have much hands-on experience with this stage of wealth transition. Additionally, the challenges encountered during this stage often have little to do with increasing revenues or decreasing costs but everything to do with managing messy human emotions, a fact traditionally ignored or dismissed by most advisors.

At a minimum, your Family Bank's governance structure will define who is to have a participating voice in your Family Bank (I address earning a voice in the Family Bank in detail in the next chapter), as well as establish a process by which your family, especially if it is large and multigenerational, is most able to effectively communicate and, to the best of its ability, continually work towards developing policies before they are needed. At the cousin consortium stage, a more rigorous process is often required in order to maintain communication and trust within the family and to educate the next generation. The ability to keep everyone not only informed but also engaged in the Family Bank as the family grows will be vital to the family members' ability to continue to work together with a shared purpose. This can include activities like regular meetings, and the recording and dissemination of the minutes of Family Bank meetings to all its members, but will depend on the unique needs of each family.

## Multigenerational Wealth and Financial Governance

The two primary assets of family wealth are family businesses, where wealth creation often originates, and financial investments, where wealth preservation is often the goal. As wealth increases, often the role of financial investing increases, and families who are new to the financial market industry, perhaps as a result of having sold their family business, or just starting to invest profits from the family business, must understand that it is one of the most competitive businesses across all industries. Sometimes, successful families enter the financial market industry with the same risk appetite they had as they built their businesses, leading to some costly mistakes. This is where a disciplined investment approach is most beneficial for families seeking to preserve multigenerational wealth.

Members of a family following the Family Bank approach, who begin by defining their shared values and vision, and assessing the family's assets, are setting the family's strategy. An investment advisor that understands this will then create an Investment Policy Statement (IPS) for the family, which translates the family's shared values and vision into financial objectives. With a clearly articulated IPS, families often find that checklist approaches—like investment products, tax minimization, control structures, and insurance products—are not the only considerations in making financial decisions. For instance, many years ago, my husband and I were approached to invest in a casino. The business was sound and our potential partners were solid, respected members of our community. However, in spite of the soundness of the investment and the potential profits, the industry did not align with our family's shared values, so we did not invest.

Developing an investment governance structure at the beginning of wealth creation is advisable, to assist with the success of both meeting financial objectives and ensuring a smooth transition to future generations. For instance, a family could create an "investment committee" within the Family Bank, which would set the guidelines for the stewardship of the family's financial assets and also be responsible for reviewing the work of any outside advisors with regards to risks taken, adherence to the investment guidelines they have been given, and their results.

This committee would also make a commitment to understanding the family's shared values and vision and manage the expectations of Family Bank members, while providing a more formal venue for strengthening communication in the family. Additionally, having any outside advisors report to the investment committee as a whole, rather than only the Family Bank leader, further prepares the Family Bank members who sit on the investment committee for their future responsibilities in financial asset management, and allows them to develop long-term relationships with outside professionals.

### The Role of Elders (Grandparents)

In North America today, our increased longevity is a delightful reality. I am reminded of this development whenever I open the newspaper, and in my personal life I am able look to my mother and my in-laws as examples of robust aging.

For a family that wishes to remain connected, elders have a valuable role to play as advisors and guides for grandchildren and sometimes great-grandchildren. This senior generation has likely begun to cede control within the family, but their wisdom and insights are significant family assets. At a time when the parents of children are inundated with the commitments of work and day-to-day family operations, elders can assist with passing along the family's shared values and traditions. All of this will help to prepare the next generation for their future roles as stewards of the Family Bank.

Philanthropy offers a marvelous starting point, one I strongly encourage, for this kind of cross-generational involvement. In working directly with grandchildren on the family's shared philanthropic goals, elders can create a nurturing environment in which their grandchildren can learn the importance of genuine caring for others and experience the satisfaction of working together on a common goal.

IN MY experience, the families and Family Banks that survive and prosper over many generations share several characteristics, like certain shared values, but another is a clearly defined governance structure, which may or may not include legal entities, for both the family and family business. Whatever committees, councils, and structures the family uses to organize itself, the goal of the Family Bank's governance structure remains the same: to create a cross-generational team in which all the generations are able to effectively work together in making decisions aligned with the family's shared values and vision.

# 11

# A TEMPLATE FOR IMPLEMENTING THE FAMILY BANK

I HOPE I have convinced you of the merits of establishing a Family Bank in the preceding chapters. Even so, you might be asking yourself, "How does my family get from here to there?" With that in mind, this chapter presents a template for implementing the Family Bank approach, drawing on examples from my own Family Bank and others.

The Family Bank approach requires effective communication built on trust, effective preparation of the Family Bank members, and a shared vision of what the Family Bank wants to achieve in the future. Along with that shared family vision comes the recognition that each generation is encouraged to become their own wealth creators while simultaneously stewarding the inherited Family Bank. In all of these areas, the Family Bank leaders have an essential role to play.

A successful Family Bank depends on each member earning a voice on the Family Bank board and on the three Ps: a shared Purpose, an agreed-upon Process, and the creation of Policies before need.

## 1. A Shared Purpose

As earlier chapters have made clear, your Family Bank's shared purpose or vision will be unique to your family. Whatever your Family Bank's goals, this is the engine that will propel your plans forward over multiple generations. Working together for the benefit of others, including future generations, provides a compelling reason for a family to remain linked. Having a shared purpose for the deployment of your Family Bank's financial assets helps manage everyone's expectations and prepares the next generation for how things will work in the future.

As Family Bank leaders, my husband and I see it as our responsibility to pass on a Family Bank that is even stronger than the one left to us by our families. Through defining our Family Bank's purpose, we focus our efforts on encouraging our younger Family Bank members to live self-fulfilled, independent lives, building our human and intellectual assets, while preparing them at the same time to become heirs and stewards of our financial assets for the human and intellectual benefit of future generations.

## 2. An Agreed-Upon Process

In the initial stages of your Family Bank, governance issues are in the infancy stages. In my family, for example, our Family Bank comprises my husband, our two sons, and me. Currently, each of us sits as a director of our Family Bank with an equal vote. We seek majority approval from directors before making any significant financial decisions. Further, rather than only depleting the financial assets, we have agreed that our Family Bank's financial capital is to be recirculated. Accordingly, we issue two kinds of loans, as follows:

### A) FINANCIAL LOANS

These are applied for as if one is applying for a loan from a traditional banking institution, say for a family member's investment in their business. In this way, next generation Family Bank members gain knowledge about the process of loans while receiving a slightly more favorable interest rate than a traditional bank would offer. Our Family Bank's assets are enhanced through the increased intellectual capital the borrower develops by going through the application process, and by the increase in our financial capital, through the interest paid on the loan.

### B) ENHANCEMENT LOANS

A Family Bank member applying for this type of loan must demonstrate that the loan will lead eventually to the member's increased independence. Education loans are a good example. Our sons do work when not attending university, but their earnings are not sufficient to support their continued education. Therefore, each of them receives a non-interest-bearing education loan they will begin to repay once they have attained full-time employment. In this way, Family Bank funds are recirculated for the education of future generations. These enhancement loans increase the human capital of our Family Bank, by supporting the younger members' pursuit of independence, as well as the intellectual capital, as each of them pursues an education.

Our Family Bank process also includes independent mentors for each of our sons. This idea came from one of our sons, in fact. During a family discussion, he asked us who would assist him and his brother in stewarding the Family Bank assets if anything should happen to us while they were still too young to do so. As a result, we guided both our sons to family friends who are willing to act as mentors, and with whom they are able to have trusted, confidential conversations. These mentors know our family well, share our values, understand the core principles of our Family Bank, and are intelligent and financially savvy.

The role of a mentor will vary from family to family. However, whatever industry your Family Bank's financial assets are predominantly in—the investment markets, food and entertainment, high tech, manufacturing, etc.—you should seek mentors who have complimentary expertise. It is also essential that the younger Family Bank members know their mentors personally and both respect and are willing to take their sage advice.

Your own family's process may or may not include structures like family corporations or trusts. Again, I would caution against setting up such structures solely to control your Family Bank's financial capital, since that approach is usually unsuccessful. You see, golden or not, handcuffs are still handcuffs. The most important thing is having a governance structure to which all Family Bank members agree, whether that is inside or outside of a legal structure.

As noted earlier, however, you can use the Family Bank approach even if you already have a complex corporate structure in place in your family. For instance, while I have some personal legal structures that have lingered from my family of origin, our Family Bank has none that relate to multigenerational planning going forward. There is no need to waste time or money dissolving these structures. In fact, they may become useful in the future governance of your Family Bank—but only if the Family Bank members agree to their use.

### 3. Policies Before Need

In my Family Bank, we have also worked on establishing policies and procedures before they are needed so that potential problems can be addressed in advance of them becoming personal and emotional. There are two significant benefits to having policies in place before they are needed. The first is that family members are prepared when potentially divisive issues arise. The second is that the skill set the family develops by creating policies, and later modifying them as necessary, helps to strengthen communication and trust. And giving each Family Bank member a voice in the setting of policies improves the likelihood of their successful implementation. Even if a Family Bank member is outvoted on a certain policy, they will have a sense of the process being fair. Also, there may be situations where a policy for the Family Bank is not created in time. In such situations, a family with an established way of working together will find it easier to develop a policy that is immediately required.

Examples of policies that should be established before they are needed are as limitless and unique as the number of families who seek to prepare them. However, one commonly used policy deals with the potential for marital breakdown and its impact on the Family Bank. This is an excellent example of where it is preferable to agree upon a policy long before it is needed. A good time to have this policy conversation with younger members is when they are beginning to enter into long-term relationships, perhaps early in their university years. After all, weddings are stressful enough. No one enjoys hearing, "Welcome to the family, dear! Now, just sign this."

The development of policies before they are needed is as important in a family business as they are to your Family Bank. Anticipating potentially contentious situations before they arise, and agreeing on solutions in advance, is a way of taking some of the emotion out of potentially explosive Family Bank issues. Additionally, the activity of creating these policies further improves communication in the family and manages the expectations of each family member, not only with regards to the specific policy being defined, but also by ensuring they understand the thought process and priorities that go into creating such policies.

## Earning a Voice on the Family Bank Board

Individuals who have earned a voice or are earnestly working towards that goal should have a say in the Family Bank's decisions. Working together in a family-friendly environment to practise negotiation skills and engage in thoughtful dialogue provides valuable life skills for individual Family Bank members and further strengthens communication within the family.

As noted earlier, each family will develop its own list of qualifications for earning a voice in the Family Bank. For purposes of illustration, here are the requirements that my husband, our two sons, and I have put in place. Each of us has agreed to:

· disagree without emotion;
· treat other family members with respect;
· remain financially independent of the Family Bank for both day-to-day needs and luxuries;
· put the needs of the family first;
· when in doubt, assume first that fellow family members are being supportive;
· be the kind of person fellow family members can trust.

This list is by no means exhaustive, but it does include requirements common to successful Family Banks.

Conducting yourself in a manner that encourages boardroom behavior supports the voice of every other Family Bank member. Family Bank members earn respect by demonstrating hard work, dedication, and expertise in their vocations, whether they are a butcher, a baker, or a candlestick maker. And stage in life is a significant factor in achieving financial independence. For example, both our sons are full-time university students who have not yet achieved independence but are working in that direction. In the meantime, their involvement in the Family Bank is critical for all of us.

Open-mindedness is another important characteristic for Family Bank members. All earned voices should be welcomed and encouraged. By the same token, members should be willing to admit when they are wrong. Some families have round dinner tables specifically to create an environment in which everyone feels they have an equal voice.

Trust is also paramount. Family members need to trust one another and also have trust in the leadership of the Family Bank. There will be times when not all Family Bank members are available to weigh in on a decision that requires an immediate response. In these situations, members must trust that Family Bank leaders will execute decisions to the best of their ability and in line with the family's shared values and vision.

## Getting Started

By now, you understand what is required for a family to successfully transition all of its assets over many generations. But you may be wondering where to begin. My best advice is to start by focusing on what should be your first priority in building a strong Family Bank: an articulation of your family's shared values. Start small, with a casual family meeting of the family members—your goal is to seek common ground and a willingness to come together on behalf of future generations of your family. Depending on your situation, this might mean beginning with some discussion between spouses before bringing other family members into the conversation. When it is time to bring in family members, I would suggest keeping the group as small as possible, for instance parents and children for the first couple of meetings, as it will simplify the process. It is often easier to reach consensus in a small group before stretching into further branches of the family, like the next generation's spouses, or grandchildren.

These initial "family meetings" do not have to be as formal as those two words sound—in fact, casual and nonconfrontational is preferred. It is far better to start small and think big. For instance, one of our family's rituals, started when our sons were quite young, was Saturday haircuts for the boys followed by dim sum at a local Chinese restaurant. As our sons are older, they now arrange their own haircuts, but dim sum is still an occasional Saturday family outing when we can all gather. Our first family meeting was held over one of these outings, and on that particular occasion, I had given them advance notice of one specific question that I would be asking. It was, "What do you think is *one value our family shares?*" When I brought the question up at lunch, it resulted in one word from each family member: "humor," "commitment," "acceptance," and "thinking." It is just that simple.

The wonderful thing about beginning in this manner is that it is fun—having fun is important—and right from the start it focuses the family on itself and the positive values that make it unique and special. I have had the opportunity to work with some remarkable families. In one instance, I was facilitating some early family meetings regarding a family's shared values when one family member suggested "stubbornness"—which can, on first blush, be seen as a negative, as in rigid, unbending, unyielding, and obstinate. But this family is none of those things, and each family member has more than earned a voice in their Family Bank: they are all educated to the best of their ability (highly in this family), and each is working or going to school and living independently of their Family Bank. In this instance, I turned the word into a positive by suggesting "steadfastness," as in loyal, reliable, stable, and established, instead of stubborn.

A word of caution here: please do not jump steps when utilizing the Family Bank approach, because doing so robs the family of the safest place to begin strengthening communication and trust within the family, the lack of which is the primary reason why succession and wealth transitions fail. I have worked with remarkable, wonderful families with solid bedrock values that have tried to skip the process of articulating their family's shared values and vision, and moved directly to assessing and dividing up the financial assets of the Family Bank. In every case, the sticking points that seemed insignificant became insurmountable. Without everyone being clear about what they are trying to achieve, unresolved issues, no matter how petty they may be, become destroyers of succession and wealth-transition plans.

Building your Family Bank may require some assistance from individuals independent of the family who have the appropriate skill set. These might come in the form of confidantes, mentors, coaches, or advisors, paid or unpaid. As an example, business leader Jim Treliving tells a story in his book *Decisions* about how his father enlisted the assistance of the local bank manager, whom the family knew well, to assist in providing a bank loan to him, which his father cosigned, in order to provide the start-up costs of his new business. The loan was handled in a very formal way: the banker, with his stern look and words, made Jim very well aware of the consequences to his father and family if he did not make his payments. The result was that loan payments were never missed and the loan was repaid as quickly as possible. However, it was not until many years later that Jim learned that the loan was actually never made by the bank. The loan was made by Jim's parents, with the banker providing a supporting role in impressing upon Jim the serious nature of this kind of contract. This is an excellent example of a Family Bank leader, Jim's father, reaching out to an individual they know and trust, an old-school banker, to provide a needed supporting role in the building of their Family Bank.

As you get started on the construction of your Family Bank, by entering into some fun family meetings, keep in mind the primary reasons why succession and wealth transition plans fail: breakdown of communication and trust within the family, unprepared heirs, and lack of a shared vision. Each step in the construction of your Family Bank addresses those issues head on, so be honest in assessing where you may need to reach out for assistance. Skipping steps only takes away valuable opportunities to strengthen your likelihood of averting the pattern of shirtsleeves to shirtsleeves in three generations.

# 12

# SELECTING FAMILY
# BANK ADVISORS

SOMETIMES WE ALL need a little help from our friends. As you work to create your family's succession and wealth-transition plan, these friends will likely be outside advisors. Professional advisors come in all shapes and sizes, from the traditional accountants, lawyers, investment advisors, and insurance agents to the new breed of advisors, under various titles and certificates that are being created, who advise on succession and wealth-transition "processes." As a CA, an Investment Advisor, a succession and wealth-transition advisor, and someone who has personally bought and sold sizeable family businesses, I understand what a key role a well-chosen professional advisor can play in the success or failure of your Family Bank.

"Data mining" is one of the twenty-first century's new buzzwords. From a business perspective, data mining is the process of analyzing large amounts of raw data and using the information to increase revenues or decrease costs. With the access afforded by our information age, organizations are surreptitiously gathering information about us all the time in order to determine what kinds of products they can sell to us. In the financial industry, those products might be insurance policies, trusts, or investment vehicles of some kind, many of them gussied up to relate to succession and wealth-transition planning.

Companies sometimes make their approaches by telephone or via an online questionnaire. They tell you they are asking for your input so that they can improve customer service. Sounds reasonable, doesn't it? Once you have spent five minutes answering a bunch of seemingly innocuous questions, they have you hooked. By the time they ask for the information they really want, your guard is down. You may want the call to end, but you are too polite to hang up, so you answer awkwardly, praying the questions will end soon. Which annual income range do you fall into? Which age range? How many dependents do you have? Etc. It is only upon reflection that you realize the questions had nothing to do with improving client service.

Instead, the information gives these service providers and product pushers a better idea about which services and products you are likely to buy. As discussed earlier, products alone cannot ensure a successful succession and wealth-transition process for your family. What they *will* do is ensure revenue for the product sellers at a cost to your Family Bank. Accordingly, it is better to select your Family Bank advisors after you have built a strong foundation by articulating your family's shared values and vision, and evaluated your family's human, intellectual, and financial assets. Completing these steps in the process will put you in the position of selecting advisors who can be charged with meeting the objectives of your Family Bank, rather than being directed by the assumed objectives of the advisors.

Once you are ready to start the selection process, it is best to examine your existing relationships first. Do you or other family members already have advisors you trust? By the time I purchased and later sold my interest in my family's professional sports and entertainment businesses, I had the professional background to negotiate my own transactions and had also developed valued relationships with other profession-als. I knew whom to turn to when I required legal expertise to execute the paperwork, and the tax transaction specialist who would ensure that the taxes were properly handled. These advisors had started their careers at the same time I did, and I knew the quality of their work. They remain trusted advisors and friends to this day. Other Family Bank members may also be in a position to make appropriate recommendations or provide valuable input on potential advisors.

Hiring advisors who are not at arm's length from the family, however, such as a member of the Family Bank or the spouse of a Family Bank member, can easily create conflict. This is another area in which having a "policy before need" in place can be very helpful. Following a process that everyone has agreed to with regard to hiring and firing, terms of reference, and compensation will go a long way towards averting any potential emotional fallout and keep Family Bank members focused on the family's shared vision. Including younger Family Bank members, even the youngest ones, in the process of hiring an advisor can be an additional learning experience for them. Through these kinds of family discussions, they will be introduced to legal, accounting, and financial jargon. This knowledge will serve them well both in their independent lives and careers and as future stewards of the Family Bank.

Relationships with outside advisors will also be most effective when all Family Bank members, not just Family Bank leaders, trust those advisors. Longtime advisors must be careful not to get stuck in a time warp, continuing to see younger Family Bank members as the children they were rather than the adults they have become. By the same token, advisors can play a key role in educating and preparing the next generation—for instance, by reinforcing family guidance that no Family Bank member should find themselves being advised to sign something they have not both read and understood. Therefore, it is useful to select an advisor who can facilitate the learning process for all Family Bank members.

Sometimes families believe they should yield to the intellect of a particular advisor. This is never wise. While the advisor may have earned a recognizable designation in their field of practice, they are rarely knowledgeable in the family's fields of expertise. Whether or not a dynamic wealth creator has had a formal education, they have created significant family wealth—human, intellectual, and financial—out of nothing. For that they have earned respect and admiration, not the airs of superiority some advisors assume based on a piece of paper hanging on their wall. Without exception, dynamic wealth creators are highly successful and of superior intellect themselves.

Some advisors also like to play up the mystique around their area of expertise, with the intention of discouraging families from questioning their counsel. Another caution here: do not be intimidated by professional designations and fancy job titles. Do not allow yourself to be sold any plan or product that you do not fully understand. Sadly, I have often found myself deciphering my clients' corporate structures and the convoluted accompanying letters from their advisors. The issue here is not that the client is unable to understand. The problem is that the advisor is unable or unwilling (I am not certain which is worse) to communicate their work in a comprehensible way.

Advisors should always create documents that you, their client and intended reader, can understand. Furthermore, never let an advisor charge you extra for time they must spend explaining their jargon-laden correspondence. This is a foolish expenditure. Besides, I think we are all tired of paying for the stadium skyboxes purchased by the employers of this type of advisor (even though I once owned the stadium!) or for new additions to their art collections.

Families who are seeking an advisor for the first time should start with some basic due diligence. First of all, ask family members and friends whose judgment you respect for referrals. Ask them not only for names but also for their observations about the advisor's communication skills and enacted values such as honesty, integrity, loyalty, trustworthiness, transparency, and confidentiality.

Once you have some names to work with, ensure that any potential advisor you consider is not only fully licensed but a member in good standing of their regulatory body. Do an internet search on the individual and the company with which he or she is affiliated. Stay alert to any hints of a company being fly-by-night. You do not want to give your trust or financial assets to someone who is here today and potentially gone tomorrow.

Be cautious of advisors of certain designations and credentials too. For instance, an elderly client of mine asked for my assistance regarding his philanthropic commitments. When I attended a meeting between my client and a representative from a well-recognized charitable organization, I learned that this charity had taken emotional advantage of my client while his beloved wife was on her deathbed, encouraging him to buy multiple insurance contracts, in loving memory of his wife, that would pay out to the charity upon my client's death.

These contracts had been entered into twenty years prior to the meeting I attended. At that meeting I learned that my client had paid, through the remittance of insurance premiums, upwards of 85 percent of the millions of dollars in total those insurance contracts would eventually pay out to the charity. That was troubling to me, but my concern did not end there. At the end of the meeting, this representative and I exchanged business cards. On the card, his name was followed by an alphabet soup of letters indicating apparent designations, none of which I recognized.

Carrying out my own due diligence, I googled his name and designations when I returned to my office. I discovered that the initials C.F.R.E. on his card stood for "certified fund raising executive." Now *there* is a designation every family being approached by the not-for-profit sector should be aware of. There are individuals out there who intentionally pursue designations to learn how to most effectively separate families from their money, to meet the fundraiser's objectives. A role that was once filled by community leaders who volunteered their time to fundraise is today performed by paid, certified employees. This is useful information to have when you are evaluating your family's philanthropic activities.

On a related point, do not be awed by job titles or confuse those titles with earned, recognizable designations. Designations like CA (chartered accountant), CIM (certified investment manager), CFA (chartered financial analyst), and CSWP (chartered strategic wealth professional) are standardized. But titles such as president, vice-president, and associate mean completely different things in different industries and companies. This is where the shock of "shock and awe" comes in, because the determining factors for many of these titles are truly shocking! So, focus on the designations and do not be afraid to ask what a particular title means or how it was earned.

Another thing to watch for—the opposite of spotting unrecognizable initials—is a potential advisor whose resumé references well-recognized educational institutions like Harvard. Of course, the implication is that the individual earned a spot at Harvard and then completed a full university degree. Perhaps that really is the case, but you need to ask the question. For example, one of the many programs offered at Harvard is a very expensive four-day seminar for family business members. Other executive business programs on their roster run for just a couple of weeks. This is a brilliant strategy on a university's part, because the fees the university collects are substantial, and the cost is worth it for advisors and other professionals looking to pad their resumés. If you are a family seeking an advisor, though, you should be careful not to take impressive-looking references like a school's name at face value.

Once you have narrowed down the field of potential advisors, the real fun begins. At least it should be fun. Your next step will be to schedule some one-on-one evaluation conversations. These meetings will require an investment of your time at the outset, but this part of the process is vital. It is your opportunity to get the information you need to make an informed decision. And effective communication will be at the heart of any long-term and mutually fulfilling relationship with an advisor.

One of the fundamental rules for those who work in the investment industry is *know your client.* It is incumbent upon investment advisors to gain a thorough knowledge of their clients, for many reasons, not the least of which is to ensure that the investments they recommend are appropriate. The reverse is also true. A basic rule for Family Bank members is *know your advisor.* It is impossible to build a trusted relationship with someone if you do not take the time to get to know him or her. This rule applies not only to investment advisors but to all advisors you use to support your Family Bank.

Many articles have been written about what to look for in an advisor, but my approach is a little different. Most advisors have strong conversational skills, so it is easy to be wooed by the first advisor you encounter. To avoid that happening, here are some things you should be wary of during your evaluation meetings with prospective advisors.

First of all, be alert to a sales pitch. A sales pitch is about convincing you to buy a product like a trust structure or insurance policy for succession and wealth-transition purposes. A sales pitch is generic, however. It does not address your Family Bank's specific objectives. In your initial conversation with an advisor, you should be doing most of the talking. Remember, this is your Family Bank you are stewarding, and the advisor must understand what it is you really want to achieve.

You should also be concerned about an advisor who sells you on the benefits of a potential plan without addressing any of the possible negative consequences. Many succession and wealth-transition advisors trained to sell their products are completely unaware of the failure rate of succession and wealth-transition plans, and the causes of such failure. For instance, be aware of any advisor who suggests a trust as a plan for the transition of financial wealth but does not bother to mention that succession and wealth-transition plans fail 70 percent of the time in spite of structures like trusts.

I would also recommend you pay attention to the tone of your conversations with potential advisors. Is the advisor helpful and instructional, or arrogant and condescending? You should never tolerate the latter. If you are wondering how to tell the difference, trust your instincts. The jargon used by advisors can be overwhelming, but sometimes it cannot be avoided. You should feel comfortable enough with any advisor to stop a meeting and ask for an explanation. Of course, any unwillingness on the advisor's part to answer a question is an indicator for you to run away and keep on running. And remember, if you receive an answer you are unable to understand, that is the advisor's fault, and not yours. Never work with anyone who cannot explain everything to you clearly.

Some industries are masterful at placing words around products to create the illusion of absolute comfort or safety. Some examples are the words "protected," "guaranteed," and "insured." Do not allow sales jargon to cloud your judgment. You should never buy any product or establish any structure unless you understand fully how the product works (and its risks) and how it will serve the goals of your Family Bank. Once you have that knowledge, you can call the product anything you want!

"High net worth" or "ultra-high net worth" are also current buzzwords, and are used to refer to clients. Some advisors believe the phrases are flattering to those individuals who qualify for the category—a sort of ego boost. In other words, clients are being defined as a group by what they can afford to pay, not as individuals and by what they need. In one extreme example, at the end of a trust seminar I engaged a fellow professional in a conversation on succession and wealth-transition planning. She was quick to share her preconceived attitudes and assumptions about inheritors and inheritances. Her comments ran along the lines of, "I couldn't care less about spoiled rich kids"—and yet there she was attending a seminar to enhance her skills to be an advisor to the parents of those individuals. The conversation was one-sided, and quickly over.

It is well understood that each of us sees the world through our own lens. Our perspectives are shaped by all of the influences on our lives, like culture, gender, age, and even financial status. In seeking advisors to assist with your Family Bank, it will be important to find those who understand your values and priorities and what it is that you want to achieve, as opposed to those who are quick to make assumptions about the kind of people you and your family must be and are quick to sell you a product sitting on their shelf.

All advisors should maintain the confidentiality of their clients' identities as well as their personal and financial information. You do not want to be associated with someone who name drops as a means of subtly enticing you to do business with them. Not only is it contrary to many advisors' codes of ethics, it is just plain wrong—and potentially dangerous. As someone who in my teenage years was tied up and held at gunpoint (not recommended) as a result of the loose lips of an advisor passing on confidential information about the contents of my family's home, I take confidentiality very seriously, and so should every advisor—and the companies they work for!

As for bragging, it comes in many forms. Is it just me, or has anyone else noticed the recent proliferation of awards being given out? As an example, I was recently contacted by e-mail, regular mail, and phone about an impressively titled investment industry award for which I had been shortlisted. I did some digging and it appeared my main qualification was that no one had complained about me to the regulatory body... gee whiz! If you meet with an advisor and they start telling you about all of the awards they've won, don't be easily impressed— what matters is how attentive they will be to *your* needs, not their own success.

The question of the advisor's fees should also be addressed during the evaluation meeting. Many people do not realize that there is great latitude in the fees charged by advisors. Never be embarrassed to ask for specific information about fees or to push to determine any hidden costs. Never make assumptions, either. One of my clients recently incorporated a holding company. He never considered asking his advisor for a fee estimate, since he knew the legal work was boilerplate: documents that the advisor could download with the click of a mouse. However, it turned out that the fee was outrageously high. What my client paid in fees could well be classified as an involuntary loss of some of his Family Bank's financial assets.

Further, when you are comparing fees between advisors, do not be fooled into thinking that paying more for something means it is better. If your needs are straightforward, consider consulting with someone who works independently or with a smaller firm. If the work involved is complicated in some way—for example, preparing tax returns for family operations in many different countries—you will have to find individuals with the requisite depth of expertise, and that will be more expensive. However, in such a case you are paying for expertise an advisor has likely spent a career building, and the work will be worth every penny of their fees.

Finally, you will want to find out whether an advisor is being incentivized, either monetarily or in some other manner, such as with internal corporate bonus points, to make certain recommendations. As an example, advisors working within bigger organizations are often encouraged to keep your assets under their roof, to cross-sell other services and products in their organization, whether or not they are the best fit for you. And keep in mind that with all the data mining they employ, they know exactly which words to use to make the sale. Additionally, some advisors are limited or restricted in the resources they have access to. As a result, their ability to provide the solution that best suits your Family Bank's needs will be focused on only what they have available to sell, which may not be what is best suited for your family's needs. For instance, an investment advisor who can only access the proprietary products of the institution they work for has far fewer options to offer their clients than one who has global access to all investments.

After all of this preliminary work, you will be in a good position to make a decision about engaging an advisor. And after weighing everything you have learned, you may decide you do not need an advisor after all. However, if you still require one, the time has come to choose one from among the prospective advisors you interviewed. To ease your concern regarding this decision, here are three things to keep in mind. The first is that you should be able to change advisors at any time. Check with the advisor you are favoring to be sure that your business and the corresponding paperwork could be easily transferred to another advisor if you wish. The second thing to remember is that there is no rush. After all, the Family Bank approach addresses the long-term goals of a family. In most instances, this means that when it comes to selecting the advisors to assist with your succession and wealth-transition planning, time is on your side. It can be a good idea to start slowly, especially if the field is new to you. There is no harm in first doing a little work using your selected advisor, taking them for a "test drive" before you are fully committed. And the third thing to remember is that despite stellar credentials, not every advisor's style, philosophy, or personality will be a good fit with you. This is normal. As with dating, follow your instincts and do not try to force a relationship.

In the end, all else being equal, you should select an advisor whose company you enjoy. I can state with confidence that there are a lot of charming, intelligent, and well-qualified advisors out there. After all, I have been happily married to one for more than twenty-five years. These same beguiling characteristics can make your relationship with your advisor so much fun. Take your time and meet as many advisors as you need to before making your well-considered decision. You may have to kiss a few frogs before you find your prince or princess, but your Family Bank will benefit enormously from it.

# CONCLUSION:

## Sharpen Your Pencil
## and Dare to Dream

ALL THE families and individuals that I work with are
thoughtful, dynamic, and passionate about their lives
and their families. From a variety of industries and stages in
life, their stories are inspirational—and the same should be said
about their succession and wealth-transition plans.

Family leaders are often genuinely worried about family harmony after they are gone. While the failure rate in the
research refers to the involuntary loss of a family's assets, no
mention is made of the number of families that fall apart over
succession and wealth-transition plans. Perhaps the number is
just too high, or the issues are just too difficult to measure in
a statistical survey because they deal with messy human emotions. However, when the Family Bank approach is used, Family Bank leaders proactively manage the expectations of the
next generation. They take great care to prepare them for how
things are going to work in the future. Even better, the next
generation will understand the reasoning behind and have a
voice in the decisions of the Family Bank. In other words, the
next generation is prepared for their future. The result is that
the eventual transition of the Family Bank to the next generation is like a warm, loving hug built on the foundation of the
family's shared values and vision.

That same spark that was ignited in you and allowed you to achieve your personal goals, whatever they may be, can be found in your family through your shared values and vision statement. Having read this book, you now know that the two biggest roadblocks on your journey towards a successful succession and wealth-transition plan are a breakdown of communication and trust in the family and unprepared heirs, and that the only way to remove those roadblocks is to start communicating and preparing. Realizing that it takes time, discipline, and thoughtfulness to reach any desired goal, one of the strengths of the Family Bank approach is that the work required to implement it takes a while, is ongoing and can be as natural as a shared family meal.

As you lie in bed tonight contemplating what it is that you want your succession and wealth-transition plan to achieve, I would suggest that you have two options. The first option is to pursue the traditionally sold route that fails 70 percent of the time, focusing on you maintaining control of your financial assets and minimizing or deferring taxes. Or you could choose option two, and incorporate the Family Bank approach into your plans and put your family on the path that successful families have followed for generations. There is no need to wake anyone up as you mull this thought over, but consider the journey you could set your family on if you sharpen your pencil and choose option two. The Family Bank approach gives families hope as their succession and wealth-transition plans evolve into their shared future dreams.

As you drift off to sleep, consider how passionately you have pursued your dreams to this point in your life, and what would be possible if some of that passion were channeled into your family's succession and wealth-transition plans. As Victor Hugo, the acclaimed French poet and novelist, put it, "There is nothing like a dream to create the future." So dare to dream as you think about your succession and wealth-transition plans, and do not let anyone, including yourself, set limits on your family and its shared future. By incorporating the Family Bank approach, what may have seemed impossible can become possible.

# BIBLIOGRAPHY

BOOKS AND PRINT ARTICLES

Aronoff, Craig E., and John L. Ward. *Family Business Governance: Maximizing Family and Business Potential.* New York: Palgrave Macmillan, 2010.

Aronoff, Craig E., and John L. Ward. *Family Meetings: How to Build a Stronger Family and a Stronger Business.* New York: Palgrave Macmillan, 2010.

Aronoff, Craig E., and John L. Ward. *How to Choose and Use Advisors: Getting the Best Professional Family Business Advice.* New York: Palgrave Macmillan, 2010.

Aronoff, Craig E., and John L. Ward. *Preparing Successors for Leadership: Another Kind of Hero.* New York: Palgrave Macmillan, 2010.

Aronoff, Craig E., and John L. Ward. *Preparing Your Family Business for Strategic Change.* New York: Palgrave Macmillan, 2010.

Aronoff, Craig E., Joseph H. Astrachan, and John L. Ward. *Developing Family Business Policies: Your Guide to the Future.* New York: Palgrave Macmillan, 2010.

Astrachan, Joseph H., and Kristi S. McMillan. *Conflict and Communication in the Family Business.* Marietta, GA: Family Enterprise Publishers, 2003.

Baines, David, and Mark Hume. "The Rise and Fall of the Griffiths Empire—Part 1." *The Vancouver Sun,* November 16, 1996.

Baines, David, and Mark Hume. "The Rise and Fall of the Griffiths Empire—Part 2." *The Vancouver Sun,* November 18, 1996.

Buettner, Russ. "Astor's Son, His Appeals Exhausted, Goes to Prison." Accessed June 21, 2013 at www.nytimes.com/2013/06/22/nyregion/astors-son-his-appeals-exhausted-goes-to-prison.html.

Canadian Institute of Chartered Accountants. *The Family Trust Guide: Family Trusts and Their Uses in Tax and Estate Planning.* Third edition. CICA: Toronto, 2006.

Carlock, Randel S., and John L. Ward. *When Family Businesses are Best: The Parallel Planning Process for Family Harmony and Business Success.* New York: Palgrave Macmillan, 2010.

Collins, Jim, and Jerry I. Porras. *Built to Last: Successful Habits of Visionary Companies.* New York: HarperBusiness, 2002.

Dalglish, Brenda. "Family Feud Sees WIC's Frank Griffiths Fired by his Mother." *The Financial Post,* September 1996.

Dickinson, Arlene. *Persuasion: A New Approach to Changing Minds.* Toronto: HarperCollins Canada, 2011.

*The Economic Times.* "Enough Reason to get Back Together." *The India Times,* March 1, 2009. Accessed June 7, 2012 at http://articles.economictimes.indiatimes.com/2009-03-01/news/28445708_1_business-families-personal-business-splits.

Fleming, Quentin J. *Keep the Family Baggage out of the Family Business: Avoiding the Seven Deadly Sins that Destroy Family Businesses.* New York: Simon & Schuster, 2000.

Frankenberg, Ellen. *Your Family, Inc.: Practical Tips for Building a Healthy Family Business.* Philadelphia: The Haworth Press, 1999.

Hausner , Lee. *Children of Paradise: Successful Parenting for Prosperous Families.* Los Angeles: Tarcher, 1990.

Hess, Edward D. *The Successful Family Business: A Proactive Plan for Managing the Family and the Business.* Westport, CT: Praeger Publishers, 2006.

Hilburt-Davis, Jane, and W. Gibb Dyer, Jr. *Consulting to Family Businesses: A Practical Guide to Contracting, Assessment, and Implementation.* San Francisco: Pfeiffer, 2003.

Hill, Crawford. Letter to his family. Published as "Bancroft Cousin's Letter: 'Paying the Price for Our Passivity,'" *The Wall Street Journal,* July 27, 2007. Accessed at http://online.wsj.com/news/articles/SB118556453898880571.

Hughes, James E., Jr. *Family: The Compact Among Generations: Answers and Insights from a Lifetime of Helping Families Flourish.* Hoboken, NJ: Bloomberg Press, 2007.

Hughes, James E., Jr. *Family Wealth: Keeping It in the Family.* Hoboken, NJ: Bloomberg Press, 2004.

Hughes, James E., Susan E. Massenzio, and Keith Whitaker. *The Cycle of a Gift: Family Wealth and Wisdom.* Hoboken, NJ: Bloomberg Press, 2013.

Kenyon-Rouvinez, Denise, and John L. Ward. *Family Business Key Issues.* New York: Palgrave Macmillan, 2005.

Kenyon-Rouvinez, Denise H., Gordon Adler, Guido Corbetta, and Gianfilippo Cuneo. *Sharing Wisdom, Building Values: Letters From Family Business Owners to Their Successors.* Marietta, GA: Family Enterprise Publishers, 2002.

Lansberg, Ivan. *Succeeding Generations: Realizing the Dream of Families in Business.* Boston, MA: Harvard Business School Press, 1999.

Latremoille, Susan, and Peter Creaghan, et al. *On The Shoulders of Atlas: A Story about Transitioning a Family-Owned Business.* Toronto: The Latremoille Group, 2010.

Lucas, Stuart E. *Wealth: Grow It, Protect It, Spend It, and Share It.* Philadelphia, PA: Wharton School Publishing, 2008.

McArthur, Emma A. "Using Trusts to Hold Recreational Property in British Columbia." Part of the conference program Trusts: Thinking Beyond Your Precedent, Pacific Business & Law Institute, June 21, 2012.

McCullough, Michael. "The Griffiths Family Saga: Line of Dissent." *The Financial Post Magazine,* May 1997.

McGowan, Luanna, Carina Weigl, and David L. Wilton. *Succession Planning Toolkit for Business Owners.* Toronto: Canadian Institute of Chartered Accountants, 2006.

Mitchell, David J., ed. "Frank Griffiths 1916–1994, Founder of Western International Communications Ltd., former owner of the Vancouver Canucks: Shooting and Scoring." *British Columbia's Business Leaders of the Century.* Vancouver: Business in Vancouver Media Group, 1999.

Nanus, Burt. *Visionary Leadership: Creating a Compelling Sense of Direction for Your Organization.* San Francisco: Jossey-Bass Publishers, 1992.

Perry, Ann. *The Wise Inheritor: Protecting, Preserving, and Enjoying Your Legacy.* New York: Broadway Books, 2003.

Rafferty, Renata J. *Don't Just Give It Away: How to Make the Most of Your Charitable Giving.* Worcester, MA: Chandler House Press, 1999.

Schneider, William, Robert Dimeo, and D. Robinson Cluck. *Asset Management for Endowments and Foundations: Improving Investment*

*Performance and Reducing Management Costs.* New York: McGraw-Hill, 1997.

Treliving, Jim. *Decisions: Making the Right Ones, Righting the Wrong Ones.* Toronto: HarperCollins Canada, 2012.

Ward, John L. *Creating Effective Boards for Private Enterprises: Meeting the Challenges of Continuity and Competition.* San Francisco: Jossey-Bass Publishers, 1991.

Ward, John L. *Perpetuating the Family Business: 50 Lessons Learned from Long-Lasting, Successful Families in Business.* New York: Palgrave Macmillan, 2004.

Williams, Roy, and Vic Preisser. *Philanthropy, Heirs and Values: How Successful Families are Using Philanthropy to Prepare Their Heirs for Post-Transition Responsibilities.* Bandon, OR: Robert D. Reed Publishers, 2005.

Williams, Roy, and Vic Preisser. *Preparing Heirs: Five Steps to a Successful Transition of Family Wealth and Values.* Bandon, OR: Robert D. Reed Publishers, 2003.

Willis, Thayer C. *Navigating the Dark Side of Wealth: A Life Guide for Inheritors.* Portland, OR: New Concord Press, 2003.

Wilson, Brian, Nancy Bullis, and Gwen Benjamin. *The Registered Charities Guide.* Toronto: Canadian Institute of Chartered Accountants, 2006.

## CORPORATE PUBLICATIONS

BDO Dunwoody LLP. *Succession Planning for the Family Farm,* 2007. Accessed at: www.bdo.ca/library/publications/tax/taxbulletins/012007.cfm.

Credit Suisse Group. *Life After an Exit: How Entrepreneurs Transition to the Next Stage.* Entrepreneurs White Paper 03, The Eugene Lang Entrepreneurship Center, Columbia Business School, 2011.

Ernst & Young Family Business Center for Excellence. *Built to Last: Family Businesses Lead the Way to Sustainable Growth,* EYGM Ltd., 2012.

Ernst & Young Family Business Center for Excellence. *Coming Home or Breaking Free? Career Choice Intentions of the Next Generation in Family Businesses,* EYGM Ltd., 2012.

Ernst & Young Family Business Center for of Excellence. *Succeeding for Generations,* EYGM Ltd., 2011.

Johnson, Howard E. *Selling your Private Company: The Value Enhancement Framework for Business Owners.* Veracap Corporate Finance Limited, 2005.

KPMG Enterprise. *Constructing a Family Constitution,* 2011.

KPMG Enterprise. *Family Business Matters,* 2012.

KPMG Enterprise. *Family Business Succession: Managing the All-Important Family Component,* 2011.

KPMG Enterprise. *Family Ties: Canadian Business in the Family Way,* 2012.

KPMG Enterprise. *Keeping It in the Family: Governance for Family Business,* 2011.

Kruger, Sarah, and Sean Foran. *Succession Stories from the Front Line: Insights and Advice for Canadian Business Owners.* Bank of Montreal, 2008.

Pricewaterhouse Coopers Family Business Services. *Making a Difference: The Pricewaterhouse Coopers Family Business Survey 2007/08,* 2007.

Walsh, Grant. *Family Business Succession: Managing the All-Important Family Component,* KPMG Enterprise, 2011.

## ONLINE RESOURCES

BCradiohistory.com. "Frank Griffiths." Accessed February 17, 2014, at http://bcradiohistory.radiowest.ca/Biographies/Griffiths.htm.

Bennest, Jack. "Frank Griffiths et al." Posting on Radiowest.ca. Accessed February 19, 2014, at www.radiowest.ca/forum/view topic.php?t=1875.

Chiner, Alfonso, and Josep Tàpias Lloret. "Top 10 Tips for Good Governance." Posting on IESEinsight.com. Accessed March 14, 2012, at www.ieseinsight.com/docImpression.aspx?id=00767.

FamilyBusinessWiki.org. Postings on family business topics, including "Deferred Compensation," "Enmeshed Families," "Governance," "Stewardship," and "Strategic Planning for the Family Business," accessed March 14, 2012 at www.familybusinesswiki.org.

Hughes, James E., Jr. "Articles and Reflections." A collection of writings available on Family Matters: The Official Website of James E. Hughes, Jr., at www.jamesehughes.com/articles.php.

Hughes, James E., Jr., Joanie Bronfman, and Jacqueline Merrill. "Reflections on Fiscal Unequals," 2000. Accessed at www.james hughes.com/articles.php.

Hutcheson, James Olan. "Building a Board of Directors: When is the Right Time?" Blog posting on FamilyBusinessWiki.org, January 31, 2013. Accessed March 6, 2013 at http://familybusinesswiki. ning.com/profiles/blogs/building-a-board-of-directors-when-is-the-right-time.

Hutcheson, James Olan. "Hidden Hurdles in Healing Families." Blog posting on FamilyBusinessWiki.org, January 31, 2013. Accessed March 6, 2013 at http://familybusinesswiki.ning.com/profiles/ blogs/hidden-hurdles-in-healing-families.

Rosenfarb, Noah. "A Guide to Building Family Legacy and Wealth." Podcast interview with James E. Hughes Jr. for Divestopedia.com, November 25, 2013. Accessed at www.divestopedia.com/2/1176/ pre-sale/emotional-aspects/podcast-i.

Schram, Carol. "Canucks' Ownership Quietly Changes Hands." Accessed June 16, 2011 at www.lcshockey.com/issues/57/ feature10.asp.

Ward, John L. "The Ten Subtle Secrets of Successful Family Businesses." Blog posting on FamilyBusinessWiki.org, December 20, 2009. Accessed June 7, 2012 at http://familybusinesswiki.ning.com/ profiles/blogs/the-ten-subtle-secrets-of.

# ACKNOWLEDGMENTS

I AM CERTAIN that a list like this is never complete. So, for anyone that I may have unintentionally missed, you are the individuals who not only listened to me but, I believe, encouraged me to talk at length on this subject matter. Thank you all for your support and enthusiasm.

Without question, I must acknowledge the truly remarkable families for whom I have had the privilege to be of service, assisting with the establishment of their succession and wealth-transition plans using the Family Bank approach. Some of these families only needed to consider a few of the concepts in this book, and in other cases I have acted as a family meeting facilitator in applying the Family Bank approach; for all, I took the utmost care to safeguard their identities and privacy. In each and every case, I am utterly awed by the strength of these families and their earnest desire to do the right thing. Without their genuine concern for their succession and wealth-transition plans to do no harm and their successful implementation of the Family Bank approach, this book would not have been written. Thank you for inspiring me to write this book and share our work with other families and their professional advisors.

Toni Cavelti, master jeweler and independant artist, and his wife, Hildegard, are successful entrepreneurs and family friends who sought my thoughts on succession and wealth-transition planning and then sparked in me the idea to make the Family Bank approach accessible to all entrepreneurial families, not just families comprised of accountants and lawyers. Thank you, Toni and Hilda, for directing my enthusiasm to delivering a useable approach for any family.

John Plul immediately understood the usefulness of the Family Bank approach and encouraged me to use my voice in communicating it. He was the very first to sit next to me and say, "You have to do this!" Great idea, thank you John.

Thank you to John Gjervan, Lynn Delahey, and Maggie Lui, fellow business team members, for your belief in the Family Bank approach and the messages contained therein–your enthusiasm and feedback inspired me to keep moving forward. Thank you all for sharing our team's vision of always putting the needs of our clients and their families first.

Gary Brookes is an Investment Advisor and a professional business associate who, through his willingness to enter into numerous succession and wealth-transition conversations, encouraged me to focus on this area of expertise. Thank you for your ongoing support, Gary.

Linda Hamer, a distinguished educator and visionary business builder, is one of the most remarkable individuals I have ever met. Aside from being the editor of my original articles in the area of succession and wealth-transition planning, Linda is the person who willingly engaged me in numerous lengthy philosophical discussions around the Family Bank approach. She is responsible for planting the seed of an idea about this book, stopping me mid-conversation to say, "This is going to be a book you have to write." Thank you, Linda, for the gentle nudge, the belief that this book should be written, and that I could do it.

Gary Nott, with the wisdom and wise counsel of a highly respected, retired Managing Partner of Deloitte & Touche in western Canada, yet actively engaged business leader, mischieviously asked my business partner, my husband, "if I could speak." Unbeknownst to him, I can, in fact, speak and it is all my speaking that crystallized the content for this book. Thank you Gary for championing my work in this area.

To David Coe and your fellow members of The Executive Committee (TEC), for bringing in an "unknown" speaker and listening so attentively to that speech. Thank you, gentlemen.

To Cathy Daminato, director of advancement at Simon Fraser University, my alma mater, for reaching into our community and bringing me back into the fold at SFU, a post-secondary institution that taught me to question the status quo in an intellectual way. Ingrained at SFU, it's exactly this kind of thinking that was foundational in writing about the Family Bank approach. Thank you, Cathy, for your support and encouragement, and for reminding me how important my SFU educational roots are.

To Chris Labonté, my publisher at Figure 1 Publishing, who took a chance and said yes to my first draft manuscript, adding "Fantastic! This is terrific! It's all there. Now, could you please rewrite it?" Chris saw the diamond in the rough and brought it into the light of day.

To Barbara Pulling, my editor, who took my second draft manuscript and did what she referred to as a "heavy edit," earning from me the nickname of "the friendly slasher." Thank you, Barbara, for brilliantly removing all the rocks from my manuscript.

To Pam Robertson and Jessica Sullivan, for copy editing and design—thank you for understanding what this book is about and weaving your expertise into the pages.

John Moonen is a friend, lawyer, and respected lobbyist in our local business community with whom I share political and Family Bank conversations. When I told John that I had written this book and it was going to be published by Figure 1 Publishing, he was the very first person to reach into his pocket and buy the first copy, even though it was still in manuscript form.

Now that was fun! Thank you, John, for your vote of confidence and your continued support.

To Elise Rees, Transaction Tax Partner, Ernst & Young, Vancouver, B.C., Market Leader Transaction Advisory Services, and decades-long friend, who has always offered me the right advice, including on transaction tax, at the right time. Thank you, Elise, for your friendship and wise counsel.

Ravi Hira and Therese Alexander have consistently offered me positive words of support, decades of friendship, title ideas, and solid legal advice. I am honored and fortunate to have such wise friends and expert legal advice in my corner. Thank you for your wholehearted support.

Bruce Barclay, a true gentleman, was my Thursday night date for dinner while I wrote this book away from home, giving me something to look forward to in between all the writing. From "Lady Hamilton" to "Mr. Barclay," thank you.

To Brian Welch, my water-ski buddy, for listening to my ramblings on the water and on the road. Ideas seem to grow better and stronger when discussed. Thank you, Brian, for allowing me to engage you in these conversations.

Gill Kassell and Julie Welch are two women with sharp wit and incisive insight. You two ladies were at the top of my list when I was trying to find a title for this book. Thank you, Gill and Julie, for your friendship, support, and seriously clever wordsmithing.

To Monica Mashal, for your thoughtful intelligence and counsel and decades of friendship. You read one of my first articles on this subject matter, long before I wrote this book and said, in a very polite way, something along the lines of, "Great, and perhaps you could be more diplomatic." As always, you were absolutely right! Thank you, Monica.

To Marion Youngberg and Pamela Thompson, young professionals at the start of their careers in the investment industry, for being willing to question the textbook and corporate-prescribed product sales solutions to succession and wealth-transition plans, and therefore willing to think outside the box and consider the Family Bank approach. I am always inspired by those professionals who put the genuine needs of their clients ahead of product sales. Marion and Pam, thank you for considering these ideas.

To Cynthia Ingram, my friend and running partner, for listening to my ramblings for years and encouraging me to write. Thank you, Cynthia, I had to start somewhere.

It almost goes without saying that I must acknowledge my grandparents and my parents for their visions for their Family Banks, and for being the role models of solid bedrock values, and also my siblings, for a lifetime of remarkable experiences.

My in-laws, George, Geraldine, Jeff, Sheryl, and Neal Hamilton, respected community leaders and farmers, also role-modeled their family's shared bedrock values and remained open to considering the Family Bank approach. Thank you all for always knowing when to tease "the city girl" and for making family meetings fun.

Donald Mackenzie is an extraordinary business builder who realized that no matter how financially successful one might be, retirement is boring, and turned his laser-sharp advice and insights towards the work that I do. Donald and I have shared endless hours of academic and practical business and wealth-transition conversations, and he was a willing and much needed sounding board while I wrote this book. I am eternally grateful for Donald's support and confidence in me and the Family Bank approach. I do not know what to call Donald: a mentor, a coach, an inspirer, a *personne de confiance*—I could chose many different titles, but if I had to pick only one, it would be a true friend.

To my sons, David and Brandon, thank you for your support, and understanding as I worked to write this book, and for your willingness to work together and with your dad and me to build our own Family Bank. Family dinners and meetings would not be as fun without your lively senses of humour! I am so proud of each of you!

Paul Hamilton is my husband and business partner, and when I suggested that it was time for me to write this book, he immediately responded with, "How can I help and what do you need?" Believing in my work with families on their succession and wealth-transition plans, and that the Family Bank approach can help other families, Paul is always at my side sharing and supporting my work and inspiring me to do my best. Thank you, Paul, for our tall sons and for being the inspired family and business leader that you are. I awake everyday grateful that I said yes when you asked me to marry you.

# INDEX